Sydney Grundy

The Glass of Fashion

An Original Comedy in four Acts

Sydney Grundy

The Glass of Fashion
An Original Comedy in four Acts

ISBN/EAN: 9783744775854

Printed in Europe, USA, Canada, Australia, Japan

Cover: Foto ©Thomas Meinert / pixelio.de

More available books at **www.hansebooks.com**

THE GLASS OF FASHION

An Original Comedy in Four Acts

BY

SYDNEY GRUNDY

LONDON
SAMUEL FRENCH, LTD.
PUBLISHERS
89 STRAND

NEW YORK
SAMUEL FRENCH
PUBLISHER
26 W. 22D STREET

THE GLASS OF FASHION.

Produced at Grand Theatre, Glasgow, March 26th, 1883; and performed at the Globe Theatre, September 8th, 1883.

CHARACTERS.

GLOBE

Colonel Trevanion	MR. LETHCOURT
Prince Borowski	MR. BEERBOHM-TREE
John Macadam	MR. J. L. SHINE
Hon. Tom Stanhope , ...	MR. C. A. SMILY
Mr. Prior Jenkyn	MR. E. W. GARDINER
Mrs. Trevanion	MISS LINGARD
Lady Coombe	MISS CARLOTTA LECLERCQ
Peg O'Reilly	MISS LOTTIE VENNE

SYNOPSIS OF SCENERY.

ACT I.— MACADAM'S CONSERVATORY, KINGSTON-ON-THAMES.

ACTS II. and IV.—TREVANION'S HOUSE IN SLOANE STREET.

ACT III.—BOROWSKI'S STUDIO.

THE GLASS OF FASHION.

ACT I.

SCENE.—*Conservatory at* MACADAM'S. *Entrances* R. *and* L. *and* R. *and* L. *at back, behind the shrubs. An- other entrance* C., *opening into a room in which, when the curtain is drawn aside, the corner of a card-table is visible. Both room and conservatory are lighted. Evening dress.* PEG *discovered looking through cur- tain* C.

PEG. Playing cards still ! When will they have done ? I can't think what's come over Nina lately. I never knew her to like cards before. But ever since we met that Polish prince she's been a different woman. How I wish Nor- man would come home.

Enter TOM, L.

TOM. Looking for me, Peg ? (*both come down*)

PEG. Tom, how late you are !

TOM. Yes, I *have* had a day of it. We're awfully busy at the Foreign Office—working overtime. I didn't get away till half-past four.

PEG. Poor dear !

TOM. These long hours knock me up. (*sits* R. *of* L. *table*) Who's here ?

PEG. Who's always here, and everywhere we go ? That odious Borowski.

TOM. What, that Polish prince ? When shall we get rid of the fellow ?

PEG. It's Lady Coombe who takes him everywhere. You know her mania for patronizing foreigners.

TOM. Lady Coombe ! (*chuckles*) Macadam's latest purchase.

PEG. Poor Mr. Macadam ! (*crosses to* L.)

3

TOM. Fancy a brewer marrying a countess. What possessed him ?

PEG. Well, you know, Tom, he can't resist a bargain.

TOM. I shouldn't think he's got a bargain there.

PEG. She was a widow when he married her.

TOM. A widow ! Oh, I see ! He got her second-hand.

PEG. Don't speak ill of your hostess. (*crosses to* R.)

TOM. I don't like Lady Coombe, and I don't like her set.

PEG. Nor I. I wish we could get out of it.

TOM. Well, I think you can. I've brought some news for you. Trevanion's back.

PEG. Tom !

TOM. I called at Sloane Street before coming here, thinking perhaps you hadn't started. But I found you'd gone and Norman just arrived. Didn't you get his telegram ?

PEG. No. We didn't expect him till to-morrow.

TOM. I said you were here, and so he's coming on to take you home.

PEG. Oh, I'm so glad he's back.

TOM. So am I, for I've announced his arrival in the paper.

PEG. You ? What paper ?

TOM. (*rising and crossing to* L.) The one I write for, *The Glass of Fashion.*

PEG. A new comic journal, I suppose ?

TOM. No, a Journal of Society. (*gives it to* PEG) Some of our fellows at the F. O. write for it, and I gave them a paragraph.

PEG. Fancy you an author !

TOM. I don't see anything to laugh at.

PEG. Oh, Tom, you won't get untidy, dear, will you, and leave off brushing your hair and wearing clean collars ?

TOM. Good gracious, Peg, why should I ?

PEG. I thought all authors were Bohemian !

TOM. Ah, that was years ago. But now Belgravian's the word. Why, dukes and duchesses write nowadays, and the Upper Ten have as much black ink on their fingers as they have blue blood in their veins. There ! (*points out the paragraph*)

PEG. (*reads*) "The husband of the beautiful Mrs. Trevanion has returned to town." "The husband of the beautiful Mrs. Trevanion "—(*pause ;* TOM *chuckles*)   Is that yours?

TOM.   I wrote it at the F. O.

PEG.   All at once ?

TOM.   Almost.   What do you think of it ?

PEG.   It's short.

TOM.   Yes, it is short.

PEG.   But——

TOM.   *Too* short, do you think ?

PEG.   Not short enough.

TOM.   Hang it, Peg, if it had been shorter there wouldn't have been any of it.

PEG.   Which would have been much better.   (*crosses to* L.)

TOM.   Don't you like it then ?

PEG.   Well, I don't want to hurt your feelings as an author, Tom, but——

TOM.   What ?

PEG.   I think we'd better not let Norman see it.

TOM.   Hang me if I write another line.

JEN.   (*off,* L.)   Charming place, really !

MAC.   (*off,* L.)   Picked it up dirt cheap.   Look at that Venus.

PEG.   Here's Mr. Macadam !

TOM.   Who's that with him ?   (*crosses to* L.)

PEG.   Oh, someone he's showing over the place.

TOM.   (*down,* L.)   He does think a lot of it !

PEG.   (*going* R.)   Yes, I believe he'll issue tickets of admission next.   He hasn't had it a month, and everyone he knows has been trotted down to inspect it.

MAC.   (*heard off*)   How much for that, now ?

JEN.   (*heard off*)   Cheap at fifty guineas.

TOM.   (*aside*)   I declare it's Jenkyn !

MAC.   (*heard off*)   Cheap, sir ?   Dirt cheap.   I gave two for it.   (*Enter* L., *followed by* JENKYN)   Well, Peg ?   (*crosses to her*)

JEN.   Your daughter, I presume ?   (*bows*)

MAC.   No, sir ; my ward.   Miss Peg O'Reilly, Mr. Prior Jenkyn ; Mr. Tom Stanhope, her young man.

TOM.   How do you do ?   (*aside to* JENKYN)   I say, not a word about me being a contributor.

JEN.   Did you say O'Reilly ?   Any relation of the Colonel O'Reilly who died in Zululand ?   (PEG *and* TOM *get back,* L.)

Mac. His younger daughter—I'm her guardian. I was poor O'Reilly's oldest friend.

Jen. Dear me !

Mac. His was a glorious death.

Jen. A sister of Mrs. Trevanion ?

Mac. You should hear Trevanion tell the story. O'Reilly died in his arms.

Jen. Quite a romance. (*aside*) This will paragraph splendidly.

Mac. Where are the others ?

Peg. Playing cards, I think. Shall I tell them you are here ?

Mac. No, don't interrupt them. Jenkyn and I have a bit of business.

Peg. Then we're in the way. Come along, Tom !

Tom. See you again, I suppose ?

Mac. Oh yes, we shan't be long.

Exeunt Peg *and* Tom, L.

Now, Jenkyn, what do you think of my place, candidly ?

Jen. Charming, my dear sir, charming. (*crosses to* R.) It's the sort of place to make a man write poetry by the yard. Pity you're not a literary man, Mr. Macadam. Splendid place for composition.

Mac. Composition ! Yes, the late owner paid three and fourpence in the pound.

Jen. Ha ! ha !

Mac. No, sir. Commerce is enough for me without literature. It's as much as I can do to look after my brewery.

Jen. Ah ! splendid body of men, sir, brewers. Most of our big brewers are political men.

Mac. Yes, I flatter myself the influence of beer upon politics is considerable. (*crosses to* R.)

Jen. What do you call your place here, Mr. Macadam ?

Mac. Fairmead ! Capital name, isn't it ?

Jenk. Capital ! and we shall make a capital article out of you for our journal. " Public Men in Private Life." Our public man next week will be Mr. John Macadam at Fairmead.

Mac. I don't object—only couldn't you use another word for public man ? You see, being a brewer——

Jen. (*laughing*) Public man ! Ha ! ha ! humorous idea ! Your views are so original ! Now what you ought to do is to start a paper of your own—something in which you could expound them. At present you give them to me—to a few intimate friends. Why not give them to the whole world? It's a duty you owe to the world.

MAC. But how? If I wrote to the *Times*, the editor would not insert my letters.

JEN. Does one shopkeeper put the superior wares of another in his window? No, sir, have a window of your own. Start an organ.

MAC. I never thought of that.

JEN. Or, better still, purchase an organ that's already started.

MAC. Second-hand, you mean; that's more in my way. If I could do it cheap.

JEN. Cheap, sir? Dirt cheap!

MAC. Then I'm your man.

JEN. And ours is the very paper for you. (*gives* MACADAM *journal*)

MAC. (*sits* R. *of* L. *table*) I've always had a taste for literature although I haven't had much to do with it. I suppose you've been in it all your life?

JEN. (*sits* L. *of* R. *table*) Certainly not, sir. I hope you don't mistake me for an ordinary professional journalist—a man who writes for his living. No, sir, we've no such person on our staff. Our contributors are mostly members of the aristocracy, who communicate piquant paragraphs about their friends and neighbors.

MAC. Oh, I see! It's an amateur affair!

JEN. My dear sir, your ordinary journalist doesn't do this sort of thing.

MAC. The *Glass of Fashion.*

JEN. The very paper for you—a shilling society journal, full of paragraphs, gossipy paragraphs, piquant *on dits.* Why, you would rule the social and political world and have society at your feet.

MAC. I should like that, certainly.

JEN. It's a splendid idea! All it wants is capital! I've brains and no capital—you've capital and no——

MAC. Sir!

JEN. And no organ. With your capital and my brains we could make the *Glass* a power in the land. Just think it over. There's a fortune in the paper.

MAC. There've been several fortunes in some papers,

and they've never come out again. (*puts paper on table*)

JEN.   But the *Glass* is bound to succeed. It will attack everybody ; therefore everybody's friends will buy it.

MAC.   Well, I'll think it over. (*rises*)   How much do you want ? Cheap, mind, cheap !

JEN.   (*rises*) Oh, a mere nothing. Say two thousand pounds. (*crosses to* L.)

MAC.   Two thousand fiddlesticks. Look here—I'll give you fifteen hundred.

JEN.   Out of the question. I couldn't think of it. (LADY COOMBE *laughs behind,* C.)

MAC.   Hush ! here's my wife. Not a word before her.

Enter LADY COOMBE *with poodle,* C., *followed by* BOROWSKI.

MAC.   (*goes up* C. *to meet her*) My dear, Jenkyn's delighted with the place—oh ! you've not seen my wife ; Lady Coombe, Mr. Prior Jenkyn, a distinguished litterateur.

JEN.   I trust your ladyship is well.

LADY C.   (R. C. *to* PRINCE) Would you hold Horace ? Thanks. (*crosses to* JENKYN) Charmed to make your acquaintance, Mr. Jenkyn. (*shakes hands*) I've heard so much of you from Prince Borowski.

MAC.   What, you know the Prince ?

JEN.   Oh dear me, yes. He's one of our contributors.

LADY C.   Indeed ! (*crosses* R. *to* PRINCE) You didn't tell me that.

MAC.   (L. C., *aside*) A prince upon the paper ? (*aside to* JENKYN) Look here ! sixteen hundred.

PRINCE.   (*to* LADY COOMBE) It is in my quality of artist I am a contributor.

LADY C.   You have so many qualities.

PRINCE.   That is why I was so anxious to paint the portrait for which you have done me the honor to sit to me. A sketch will appear in the journal.

LADY C.   It is too flattering, Prince. (JENKYN *going off*)

PRINCE.   To flatter Lady Coombe would be impossible.

LADY C.   Mr. Jenkyn, you won't go without letting me introduce you to Mrs. Trevanion ?

JEN.   (L.) Certainly not ; I shall be delighted. (LADY COOMBE *goes up* C.)

MAC. Oh, he's not going yet. I haven't shown him-half over the place. By-the-bye, have I shown you my new oriel window? It's in the billiard room.

JEN. No.

MAC. Oh, my dear fellow, come along. (*goes* R.)

LADY C. Au revoir!

MAC. Au revoir—for the present.

JEN. (*going* R. *with* MACADAM) You will think over the matter?

MAC. Yes, I'll think it over; but I don't like the title.

JEN. The *Glass of Fashion?* It's a splendid title.

MAC. Yes, but don't you see—me being a brewer, don't you think the *Glass*—eh? Isn't it a bit too——

JEN. Ha! ha! What a fund of humor! (*Exeunt* MACADAM *and* JENKYN, R.

LADY C. (*who has sat down* R. *of* L. *table*) Lucky again at cards to-night, Prince. You are fortune's favorite.

PRINCE. (*sits* L. *of* R. *table*) It pains me greatly to have won so much, but *you* are not the loser.

LADY C. I owe you a thousand.

PRINCE. Mrs. Trevanion lost as much to you.

LADY C. Poor Nina! How unfortunate she is!

PRINCE. Happily she is rich and will not feel the loss. Sole heiress of her father, the late Colonel O'Reilly, she is to be envied.

LADY C. She ought to be well off. The estates are entailed, so she derives the entire income from them. Why she should always seem so pressed, I can't imagine.

PRINCE. Has she not paid you?

LADY C. Only five hundred pounds. For the rest she's given me her I. O. U., otherwise *I* should have paid *you*, Prince. You know I never bother my husband about these matters.

PRINCE. (*rises; crosses to* LADY COOMBE) Unhappily I've heavy liabilities to meet this week. I do not always win, and I have a large sum to pay to-morrow; I was about to ask you if it would be convenient to let me have the thousand.

LADY C. Now? To-night?

PRINCE. To-morrow at the latest.

LADY C. It's impossible! Unless I break my rule and ask Macadam.

PRINCE. No need to do that, Mrs. Trevanion ought to pay her debts !

LADY C. Poor Nina !

PRINCE. Chut ! Here she comes. Better ask her now.

Enter NINA, C. ; PRINCE leads her down to chair L. of R. table.

LADY C. (*rises, crosses to NINA*) Nina dear, one moment.

PRINCE. Ah, you have private matters to discuss. I will withdraw myself. (*bows and goes up*)

LADY C. (*to PRINCE*) Would you hold Horace ? Thanks ! (PRINCE *takes poodle and exit L.*)

NINA. (*sits R.*) What is it ? (*anxiously*)

LADY C. My dear child, it is most distressing to have to put you to any inconvenience, but I must really ask you to redeem your I. O. U. My losses this week have been terrible.

NINA. And mine ! What am I to do ?

LADY C. You know I have waited a long time, my dear, and the amount gets larger every night.

NINA. I *must* go on now. I *must* win it back.

LADY C. Cannot you ask your husband ?

NINA. (*impatiently*) Oh ! Norman ! Besides, he isn't home yet.

LADY C. Then there's no alternative. I must *part* with your I. O. U.

NINA. Don't let it go out of your possession. Anything but that.

Enter SERVANT, R.

SERV. Mr. Macadam's asking for your ladyship. Colonel Trevanion has arrived.

NINA. (*rises and crosses to L.*) My husband !

LADY C. The Colonel ! I will come down instantly.
        Exeunt LADY COOMBE and SERVANT, R.

NINA. (*pacing up and down, watched by the PRINCE amongst the shrubs at back*) My husband here ! What will become of me ? I hoped to have got out of all my difficulties before he came. How can I tell him of them— him, of all men—with his ideas ! Norman is so old-fashioned, and we are always disputing about money. To begin again directly he comes home ! Oh, I can't ask him—it's impossible. (*drops into chair* R. *of* L. *table, leans her head upon her hands*)

PRINCE. (*who has got rid of poodle at back ; aside*) Now is my opportunity to play the friend in need. There is some skeleton in the Trevanion cupboard. If I could only find out what it is.

MAC. (*heard off* R.) Cheap ! I should think it was ! You haven't half seen it yet.

TREV. (*heard off* R.) If you don't mind, I'd rather see my wife——

MAC. (*off* R.) Of course ! What was I thinking of.

PRINCE. (*aside*) Peste ! I have lost my opportunity.

Re-enter MACADAM, *followed by* TREVANION *and* LADY COOMBE.

MAC. Here he is, Nina, home again at last.

NINA. Norman !

TREV. My darling !

MAC. What's become of Jenkyn ? (*Exit,* R.)

NINA. You're back sooner than you expected.

TREV. Yes, but not so soon as I hoped.

NINA. And I.

LADY C. Colonel, let me introduce you to my friend, Prince Borowski. (NINA *sits* R. *of* L. *table ; aside*) . A distinguished Pole ; you know my sympathy with his unfortunate country.

PRINCE. (*crosses* to TREVANION) I am delighted to meet Colonel Trevanion, for I need hardly say I know you well by reputation (*bows*)

TREV. And I you (*crosses* to LADY COOMBE, R.; *aside*) Then he's left Poland ?

LADY C. Oh, some years.

TREV. (*crosses to* NINA, L.) Poland's not so unfortunate after all.

NINA. (*rises*) You've heard of Prince Borowski ?

TREV. At the clubs. His luck at the card-table is a proverb. (NINA *sits*)

Re-enter JENKYN *and* MACADAM, R.

MAC. I say, Trevanion, here's Jenkyn dying to be introduced to you.

JEN. What, is this the celebrated——

MAC. Yes, the man whose name was upon everybody's lips over that dreadful affair at Rorke's Drift.

JEN. Sir, I am proud to meet you. (*crosses to* TRE-
VANION. TREVANION *merely bows*)

LADY C. Poor dear O'Reilly! Capital officer. (*rises*)
And so he died in your arms? (*eye-glass*)

JEN. Eh? (*aside*) Where's my note-book?

TREV. I rendered him the last service one soldier can
render another, madam, that was all.

MAC. Tut, tut, my dear fellow, you hide your light
under a bushel. It was a splendid thing—bullets raining
like hail, assegais here and assegais there, and those grin-
ning blackamoors howling and shrieking, and he kept the
lot at bay, fighting like a devil until he carried O'Reilly
to a place of safety.

TREV. Alas! only to receive his last words.

JEN. (*with note-book*) And they were——

TREV. Strictly confidential.

JEN. Oh! (*turns off*)

NINA. Who is that man?

TREV. I haven't an idea. (*sits* L. *of* L. *table*)

LADY C. (*rises*) Prince! I don't see Horace! What
have you done with him?

PRINCE. What have I done with Horace? Let me
think. Ten thousand pardons, Comtesse, but I cannot
recollect.

LADY C. You've mislaid Horace? (*all look about*)

Re-enter PEG, L. C., *at back, followed by* TOM *carrying
poodle.*

PEG. Looking for Horace? He's all right!

TOM. I've got him.

LADY C. (*crosses to* C. *and takes poodle*) My poor
darling! If anything had happened to him, I should
never have survived it.

PRINCE. (*going* R., *aside*) Peste! I was hoping the
little brat was lost forever.

MAC. (*to* JENKYN, *who has buttonholed him, coming
down* C.) Certainly, Jenkyn, certainly—with pleasure.
(*introduces him to* NINA). Mrs. Trevanion—Mr. Prior
Jenkyn, editor of the *Glass of Fashion.*

JEN. No doubt you have seen the paper.

NINA. (*who has risen*) No—I've not had that pleasure. (*goes up to* PEG)

TREV. What is it? Something new?

JEN. Haven't *you* seen it?

LADY C. (*crosses from back to* R. *of* L. *table*) Oh, it is full of the naughtiest innuendoes. If you wish to see the follies and scandals of the day——

MAC. (*interrupting her*) You must look in the glass. (LADY COOMBE *sits and looks at him through eye-glass*)

NINA. (*at table* L. *of* R.) I hadn't even heard of the paper! (*sits*)

PRINCE. (*sits at table* R. *of* L.) Then you've not seen the paragraph which has set everybody talking?

NINA. No! What is it about? (JENKYN *points it out to* TREVANION)

TREV. (*reads*) "The rage for gambling among the fair sex seems to be on the increase. A lady well known in society is reported to have lost more than she can conveniently pay. Additional piquancy is lent to the rumor by the fact that her husband is in sublime ignorance of her embarrassment."

MAC. Poor devil!

NINA. (*aside to* PRINCE) Why did you mention it?

PRINCE. It was the best way to disarm suspicion.

LADY C. The paragraph is the talk of the town.

JEN. Yes, I flatter myself it's created a sensation.

MAC. The *Glass* is in everybody's mouth.

JEN. (*to* TREVANION) What do you think of the title? Appropriate, isn't it?

TREV. Very appropriate! A glass reflects, and this seems to contain nothing but reflections.

JEN. (*crosses to* PEG) Glad you like it. What do you think of it, Miss O'Reilly?

PEG. I don't think it at all appropriate. A glass casts its reflections to your face. These reflections are all behind people's backs.

JEN. You're severe.

TREV. So is Mr. Jenkyn, if the few paragraphs I glanced at are any criterion.

MAC. (*to* TREVANION) Don't frighten me, Trevanion. I'm going to see *myself* in the *Glass* shortly. That's what Jenkyn came about. He wants to describe my place. We've been all over it except the picture gallery. (*to* JENKYN) You haven't seen them.

TREV. (*rises*) Then you're engaged. I should have liked a few minutes' conversation with you. (SERVANT *appears*, C.)

MAC. By all means. My wife'll do the honors.

LADY C.   You forget, Mr. Jenkyn's had a journey and would perhaps take some refreshment. (*rises.* SERVANT *exits* C. *Takes* JENKYN'S *arm*) For my part I find pictures very fatiguing. Prince, would you hold Horace? Thanks. (*Gives the poodle to* PRINCE *and exits with* JENKYN.)

PRINCE.   (*to* TOM) Would you hold Horace? Thanks. (*gives poodle to* TOM, *and exits* C. *with* NINA)

TOM.   Oh, hang it all! (*to* PEG *on steps*) Would you hold Horace? (*gives* PEG *poodle*)

PEG.   Thanks. (*exit with* TOM, C.)

MAC.   Now, my boy! (*sits* R. *of* L. *table*)

TREV.   (*sits* L. *of* L. *table*) Macadam, I want to talk to you about Peg. That is the reason I've made such haste home. I was determined to be back before her birthday. Next week she'll be twenty-one and I have to give you an account of my stewardship.

MAC.   It's only a matter of form. I know the money's all right, but as trustee under the settlement, you see I'm bound——

TREV.   Of course! Thank goodness we shall soon be rid of this secret, and there will be an end to the misunderstanding it has caused between Nina and myself.

MAC.   It's been a tough job, hasn't it?

TREV.   I little dreamt, when poor O'Reilly made me his confidant, how difficult a part I should have to play. I had no time to think.

MAC.   I suppose he didn't tell you till the last.

TREV.   Then he told me everything, and made me promise that the secret should be kept as long as possible from both his children.

MAC.   He made me promise the same thing when I was appointed trustee.

TREV.   The last word he heard on earth was my assurance that the cruel story should be kept from Nina as long as possible.

MAC.   He didn't tell me the whole history, and I've not cared to talk about it since. Who was the mother? Dancer, wasn't she?

TREV.   Yes; an opera dancer whom he met and fell in love with at Vienna.

MAC.   Pity he didn't marry her at first.

TREV.   She was already married!

PRINCE *appears*, C., *behind shrubs, smoking cigarette, with poodle ; he listens.*

MAC. Ah ! he didn't tell me that !

TREV. Her husband had deserted her, but she was not divorced, and so, of course, O'Reilly couldn't marry her. A few months after Nina was born the scoundrel was killed in a duel, and O'Reilly married the widow. Peg, being legitimate, of course comes in for the estates.

MAC. Whilst poor Nina——

TREV. Has not even the right to her father's name !

PRINCE. (*aside, at back*) Ah, the skeleton !

MAC. Why didn't he make a will and put things straight ?

TREV. The property's entailed—he had no power to alter the succession.

MAC. Of course he hadn't—no. Poor Nina !

TREV. She was his favorite, and his last agony was lest she should learn the truth.

MAC. It must come out next week. By Jove, how glad I am not to have had another man to deal with. If anybody else had married Nina and I'd had to tell him— Phew !

TREV. Thank heaven, nobody knows it yet except us two.

PRINCE. (*aside*) Us three, *mon ami*, us three ! (*disappears*, L.)

MAC. And we've got out of it cheap, my boy, dirt cheap. (*rises*) But, I say, you've not seen my Vandyke ; I must show you that. Picked it up last week in the Old Kent Road.

TREV. (*rising*) What is the subject ? (*both going*, R.)

MAC. I can't quite make out. But, after all it's not the subject—it's the execution. Dirt cheap at a tenner.

TREV. A Vandyke at that price ?

MAC. Talk of a shay d'over, damme, it's shade all over.
Exeunt, R.

Re-enter PRINCE, L., *with poodle.*

PRINCE. Am I to carry this about all the night ? If the room is too close for him, am I his nurse to take him promenades ? Bah ! He has four legs of his own. Let him promenade himself ! (*puts poodle down*, 2 R. L.) And so the husband has returned just when I was begin-

ning to make progress. Mrs. Trevanion will confide in
him, he will pay the money, and there will be an end to
her difficulties—those difficulties I have brought about
with so much trouble. But can he pay? If half they
say is true, he is himself embarrassed. *Tant mieux.* He
will be the more useful to me. (*crosses to* R).

Re-enter NINA, C., *goes down,* L.

NINA.   I can't rest in that room.   Each time Lady
Coombe looks at me she seems to ask me for the money.
(*sees* PRINCE, *whose eyes are fixed on her*) Prince!
    PRINCE.   Madame, you seem distressed!
    NINA.   That dreadful paper!
    PRINCE.   Ah, that is all!
    NINA.   Tell me the truth.   Do they mean me?
    PRINCE.   Impossible to say.   The cap fits so many.
    NINA.   What am I to do?   I am at my wits' end and
shall have no rest until the money's paid.   You are a man
of the world, Prince—give me your advice.   Is there no
way out of my difficulty without speaking to my husband?
    PRINCE.   Do not do that, madame.   Husbands in these
affairs are undesirable.   Believe me, as your friend, it
would be the cause of more unhappiness in a home in
which I fear there is too much already.
    NINA.   Ah! (*sits* R. *of* L. *table*)
    PRINCE.   But do not be anxious.   It makes my heart
bleed to see you so distressed.   These little difficulties
are not so uncommon, and there are ways out of them.
Money is always to be borrowed.
    NINA.   But I have borrowed all I can, and have no
other friend of whom I could ask such a service.
    PRINCE.   We do not always know our friends, madame;
sometimes we look for them vainly in the clouds when
they are at our feet.   (*kneels and kisses her hand*)

Re-enter PEG, C.; *they start away from one another.*
    PRINCE *crosses to* R., NINA *rises.*

PEG.   Nina, they're wondering what's become of you.
    NINA.   I came to look for Horace.   Lady Coombe
seemed so concerned lest the Prince should lose him
again.   (*goes up to* PEG)
    PRINCE.   Horace!   I had forgotten all about the little
devil.   Horace!   My little pet, where are you?   Ah, you

want a little prussic acid ; you shall have a little prussic acid. (*Exit*, L.)

PEG. Nina, what is the matter ? I have been watching you all the evening. Something has happened. Tell me what it is.

NINA. (*sits on garden seat*) Nothing of any consequence.

PEG. It is of consequence when it makes you look so wretched, when it makes secrets between us who never had one in our lives before, and when it makes you confide in those who've no right to your confidence.

NINA. You mean the Prince ?

PEG. What was he saying when I interrupted you ?

NINA. He was only giving me his advice.

PEG. What right has he to give you his advice, and how much is it worth ?

NINA. (*rises ; crosses to* L.) Nonsense, Peg ; the Prince is a man of the world and you are a mere child. (*sits* R. *of* L. *table*)

PEG. I am your sister.

NINA. That's no reason I should tell you everything.

PEG. A sister is a better confident for a wife than a man of the world is, unless he's her husband. If you're in any trouble, why don't you speak to Norman ?

NINA. Oh, Peg dear, I daren't.

PEG. Is it so bad as that ?

NINA. No—you misunderstand me—but you know how old-fashioned Norman is.

PEG. I know how good he is. Perhaps that *is* old-fashioned.

NINA. And how annoyed he gets over *trifles* no reasonable man would give a second thought to.

PEG. I don't believe it *is* a trifle, Nina. Something has altered you altogether lately ; I'm not the sister to you that I used to be. Something has come between us ; and I can't help suspecting——

NINA. What do you suspect ?

PEG. Don't ask me. Trust in me. Don't leave me to suspect ; *tell* me what's the matter. I can't bear to go about watching and suspecting, when you know I love you more than anybody in the world, except Tom. Nina darling, confide in me as you used to do.

NINA. (*arms round her*) Oh, Peg dear ! I'm in such trouble,

2

PEG.   I knew you were.   Tell me what it is, and see if I can't help you.

NINA.   I'm ashamed to tell you.   Besides, you couldn't possibly assist me.

PEG.   Couldn't Norman ?

NINA.   Yes, Norman might !

PEG.   Then tell him, Nina, and I won't bother you any more.

NINA.   Peg ! (*kisses her*)   You were always my good angel.   I will speak to Norman.

PEG.   Darling !

NINA.   But how can I get him by himself ?

PEG.   Oh, if that's all, I'll manage that.

MAC.   (*off*, R.)   There, what do you think of that ?

TREV.   (*off*, R.)   It's big enough !   The Läocoon, isn't it ?   (PEG *and* NINA *go up back*)

Re-enter MACADAM *and* TREVANION, R.

MAC.   I don't know what coon it is, but he was a gone coon to me at Smith's sale for a fiver ; dirt cheap I call it.

Re-enter TOM, C.

TOM.   I say, Macadam, going to have a sale ?

MAC.   Sale ? Hang it, no ! I've only just bought the place.

TOM.   Here's Jenkyn making a regular inventory of the furniture.

MAC.   Oh, that's all right.   He's doing it for the *Glass*.

PEG.   Hadn't you better help him ? (*taking his arm*)

MAC.   Well, come along, my dear, we'll see what we can do.

TOM.   There's really no necessity.   He's helped himself to everything already. (*Exit, following* PEG *and* MAC-ADAM, C.)

TREV.   Shall we go with them ?

NINA.   No—I want to speak to you.   Can't you give me a minute ?

TREV.   As many as you please.   You know I'd give you anything you asked.

NINA.   Anything ?

TREV.   In my power.

NINA.   I don't like to talk about momey matters directly you come home, but I can't help it.

TREV.   You want money ?   How much ?

NINA. A thousand pounds.

TREV. A thou—Nina, be serious.

NINA. It isn't very much.

TREV. (*sighs*) Just now it is a great deal. It isn't a pleasant subject, but as you've broached it I may as well tell you at once that I am in difficulties and we can't keep on at our present rate much longer. (*sits* L. *of* R. *table*)

NINA. In difficulties? We don't live beyond our income, and I'm sure I have nothing that isn't necessary for your wife.

TREV. However that may be, I'm seriously pressed for ready money, and, to be frank, I should prefer that we went to some quiet place and retrenched.

NINA. Leave London in the height of the season! (*crosses to* TREVANION) What are you hiding from me, Norman? Have you been speculating?

TREV. I am not likely to gamble. It is a vice I detest.

NINA. Then how can you be short of money? My fortune is a large one. (*crosses to* L.) You have the sole control of it.

TREV. (*rising*) I'm not speaking of your fortune, but of my income.

NINA. You needn't touch your income. All I want is one thousand pounds of my own money.

TREV. (*crosses to* NINA, L.) I have explained to you that for the present your money is tied up.

NINA. But I don't understand.

TREV. It is a legal question.

NINA. So you always say. (*crosses to* R.)

TREV. What do you want with this money? If it be for bills, give them to me and I will see what I can do.

NINA. Norman, I must decline to have an inquisition held on my expenditure. Cannot you trust me? (*crosses to* TREVANION)

TREV. Trust you, my dear? You know that I trust you implicitly.

NINA. Will you give me a cheque to-morrow?

MAC. (*outside,* C.) Nonsense! it's no use asking me—ask him yourself.

TREV. I'll see what I can do.

Re-enter MACADAM *and* JENKYN, C.

MAC. Trevanion, Jenkyn here wants to put you in the *Glass.*

Re-enter PRINCE, L.

JEN.   To include you in our series.

TREV.   What, Beauties of Society ?

Re-enter LADY COOMBE, *with poodle,* C., *comes down to* R. *table.*

MAC.   No, no—your wife's in that.

JEN.   The Prince will make a splendid portrait of her.

TREV,   Prince Borowski contributes to this journal ?

PRINCE.   Only as artist.

MAC.   He does the pictures.

JEN.   (*showing sketch*)   This is No. I.

Re-enter PEG *and* TOM, C.

LADY C.   Let me see, who is that ?

JEN.   To avoid mistakes, the name is printed legibly below.   No. , Mrs. Vandyke Brown.

NINA.   A speaking likeness !

PRINCE.   (*crosses to table,* R.)   It is on the expression that I pride myself.

LADY C.   You've evidently observed that poor Mrs. Brown has none.   (PRINCE *bows grimly*)

PRINCE.   The criticism is severe, but just.   Mrs. Brown makes a portrait, but she does not make a picture.   But when I come to No. 4, Mrs. Trevanion——

TREV.   You will have to draw either from your imagination or your memory.

PRINCE.   Am I to understand——

TREV.   Mrs. Trevanion will not sit for you.

ALL.   Not sit ?

NINA.   But I have promised—what is your *objection ?*

TREV.   I *object* to my wife's portrait being *bought* and *sold.*

PRINCE.   The beauties of society without Madame ! It is a court without a queen.

TREV.   You must find a substitute.

PEG.   (L.)   I suppose *I* wouldn't do ?

MAC.   (*approvingly*)   Peg !

TOM.   (*amazed*)   Peg !

PEG.   Oh, wouldn't it be nice ?   Just fancy *me* a beauty of society !

JEN.   Unfortunately there is no demand for unmarried ladies.

PRINCE.   (*crosses to* PEG)   But I shall be proud to

undertake the task of sketching Miss O'Reilly—if Mr. Stanhope is agreeable.

PEG. Oh, he doesn't mind.

TOM. It would be rather fun to see Peg on the bookstalls.

PEG. Just out, " The beautiful Miss O'Reilly," price one shilling. When will you sketch me, Prince ?

PRINCE. Make your own appointment.

MAC. Jenkyn, I'll give you eighteen hundred ! There !

JEN. My dear sir, I couldn't think of it !

MAC. Don't run away like that. Say *nineteen* and I'll give you a cheque now. (*go up talking*)

LADY C. Going already ?

Meanwhile TREVANION *has spoken to* NINA ; NINA *rises and goes to* LADY COOMBE ; TREVANION *to* MACADAM.

MAC. Nonsense, my dear fellow. Your wife's not seen my pictures. Chose the frames myself. Dirt cheap, considering the size of 'em. (*talks to* TREVANION)

LADY C. (*to* NINA) Then I shall see you to-morrow.

NINA. Probably ; if not——

LADY C. I must part with the I. O. U.

NINA. To-morrow, then.

LADY C. I shall expect you. (NINA *joins* PEG ; *they exeunt* L.)

TOM. Stop, Peg ; wait for a fellow—hang it !

LADY C. I'll come down to the grounds and see you off. (*takes* TOM'S *arm, stops ; to* PRINCE) Would you hold Horace ? Thanks ! Now, Mr. —— (*exit* L. *with* TOM. TREVANION *crosses to* L.)

PRINCE. Good evening, Colonel. Charmed to have met you. I trust we shall have many opportunities of bettering our acquaintance. (*offers his hand*)

TREV. That is unnecessary, Prince. I know you better than you think already. (*bows and exits,* L.)

PRINCE. (*looking after him*) You will not take my hand. Ah, you shall change your tone. You will not be my friend, then I will be your enemy.

MAC. (*to* JENKYN) Look here—I'll give you the two thousand pounds.

JEN. Sir, the *Glass* is yours, and you've got it cheap. (*shakes hands*)

MACADAM *takes the " Glass " and comes down* R.

PRINCE. (*taking* JENKYN *up*) Jenkyn—a leetle paragraph. (*music*)

MAC. (*flourishing paper*) The *Glass* is mine. I shall be a power in the land. I shall rule the social and political world and have society at my feet.

PRINCE. Would you hold Horace? (*quick curtain*) Thanks! (*puts poodle in* MACADAM'S *arms and walks off* L.; *arm in arm with* JENKYN)

END OF ACT I.

ACT II.

SCENE.—*A library at* TREVANION'S. *Doors* R. *and* L. JENKYN *discovered looking about the room.*

JEN. Snug little place. Reminds me of the Duke's. (*drops a card*) No, it doesn't look natural there. (*picks it up and puts it on desk at back*) That's better. Always as well to drop a card—no knowing who may pick it up. (*seeing some letters on table*) Hulloa! he hasn't opened his letters yet! (*examines them*)

Enter SERVANT, R. JENKYN *business with letter.*

SERV. The Colonel will be with you directly, sir.

JEN. (*turning*) Ah, ah, thank you. Here, one minute. Been with the family long?

SERV. I beg your pardon.

JEN. Master and missus get on pretty comfortable, eh?

SERV. (*crosses to door*, L) Master'll see you directly. You can ask him yourself. (*exit*, L.)

JEN. That girl's not lived in good families. I'll just take a note or two. (*pulls out book, looks down*) In front of the fireplace is an exquisite rug of—dash it all, wonder what the animal is. (*examining corner of rug*) Between the windows is a splendid picture of—hang it, I forgot to ask the servant who that was. Wonder who's the artist. (*mounts chair and examines picture*) Don't say!

Enter MACADAM, L.

MAC. Ouf, there you are. They told me at the office you were here.

JEN. (*looks round, still on chair*) This is an unexpected meeting.

MAC. It's a meeting at which you've taken the chair. What the devil are you doing?

JEN. (*still examining picture*) Working up Colonel Trevanion at Home.

MAC. But Colonel Trevanion isn't at home up there.

JEN. Want to describe his pictures, etc. Doesn't do to stand on ceremony in these matters, you know.

MAC. Stand on ceremony! you're not particular what *you* stand on. Get down and come here. (*goes* C. JENKYN *gets down, and comes to* MACADAM) This was addressed to the proprietor of the *Glass of Fashion.* I've just got it.

JEN. Oh, a postcard!

MAC. Yes, here's a nice thing! (*reads*) "To the Proprietor of the *Glass of Fashion.*—Sir, Your infamous journal has grossly insulted me. I shall have the pleasure of waiting upon you at the office this morning with a horsewhip.—John Jones." What have you been saying about John Jones?

JEN. Jones—Jones—oh, ah, yes, we had a par. hinting he had an unfortunate habit of putting the silver spoons in his pocket when he dined out.

MAC. (*sits* R. *of table*) How ever could you print such a statement?

JEN. My dear sir, I was astonished when I read it. I can t imagine how it could have got in.

MAC. You must call on him and apologize.

JEN. My dear sir, it isn't the editor he wants to see, it's the proprietor. You'd better go.

MAC. What, and be horsewhipped?

JEN. Well, commercially, it wouldn't be a bad thing. You could summon him—the case would be exposed, and it would be a splendid advertisement for the paper.

MAC. And let everybody know that I'm the proprietor. Not me, thank you. I didn't bargain for this sort of thing when I bought the paper. I shall expect to see myself with a black eye every time I look in the *Glass.* You go and tell him we'll apologize, and stop him coming to the office.

JEN. Apologies won't increase our circulation.

MAC. No; but a horsewhipping would increase mine. I came directly I opened this. I thought you ought to

see it.   Here are some more addressed to the proprietor,
but they are about advertisements.   Take them.   (*rises
and gives letters to* JENKYN)

JEN.   Here's one you haven't opened.   (*gives a letter
back to* MACADAM, *crosses to desk at back*)

MAC.   Eh? so there is   (*opens letter ; sits*)   Good
heavens, another lawyer's letter.   "Sir,—I am instructed
by my client, Mrs. Nemo, to call your attention to a libellous paragraph in your last issue.   Unless immediate
compensation for the injury caused be made, I shall apply
for a criminal information.   I would suggest an apology
in your next number and a solatium of two hundred
pounds."   (*rises and crosses to* JENKYN)   What the devil
have you been saying about Mrs. Nemo.

JEN.   (*rises*)   Nemo !—Nemo !—Ah, I remember.
There was a paragraph hinting that she had committed
bigamy.

MAC.   Good heavens, man, you must be mad to put
such a thing in.   (*sits* R. *of table*)

JEN.   I never saw it till it was in print.   I can't imagine how it got in.

MAC.   You've let me in for a nice thing with this pre-
cious paper.   You told me I should have society at my
feet.   Gad, I shall have society at my back.

JEN.   We must have a little gossip, you know, or you'll
be beaten by your contemporaries.

MAC.   Damme, at present it looks more like being
beaten by my readers.   No more of this sort of thing, if
you please, Mr. Jenkyn.

JEN.   My dear sir, now I know your views I'll take care
it doesn't occur again.

MAC.   Mind it doesn't, or I shall begin to think I've got
a bad bargain.   If I get out of this lot for two hundred
pounds, it will be cheap, dirt cheap.

Enter TREVANION, R.

TREV.   (*to* JENKYN, *coldly*)   Good-morning.   Ah,
Macadam !   (*crosses to him and pushes him into seat* R.
of table and crosses to fireplace)   You wish to see me ?

JEN.   Yes, about the matter I mentioned yesterday.   I
want to do you among my series of "Public Men in
Private Life."

TREV.   Private life ceases to be private life if you make
it public.

MAC. I am going to be in the series.

JEN. I want to give the public an idea of your home. Style of living, kind of furniture, and that sort of thing.

MAC. He knows how you stood before the fire of the enemy. He wants to show them how you stand before your own.

TREV. (*crosses to* C.) I object to stand on my hearth-rug for the public to stare at me at so much a head.

JEN. But, my dear sir, our public is not an ordinary public. Ours is not a sixpenny journal. We employ no professional journalists, sir; the aristocracy read this paper and the aristocracy write it.

TREV. I know your paper is an amateur affair.

JEN. My dear sir, amateur! Why a duke must know how to write about dukes better than a professional scribbler.

TREV. And Colonel Trevanion must know better how to write about Colonel Trevanion than Mr. Jenkyn. When I want to appear in your journal I'll supply you with the matter. (*rings bell*)

JEN. Just what we want. Now give us the materials.

TREV. To-day I'm busy. Good-morning, (MACADAM *rises*) Mr. Jenkyn. You going too, Macadam?

MAC. I'm coming back directly. I've arranged to meet my wife here. Must go now, I have to call at my solicitor's.

JEN. (*aside to* MACADAM) Tell him it's your paper.

MAC. Not for the world. (*drags* JENKYN *off* L.)

TREV. (*seeing card on desk, picks it up*) One moment, Mr. Jenkyn, I think this belongs to you.

JEN. Oh, oh—er—yes, I must have dropped it by accident. Thank you. (*exit,* L.)

TREV. Hang his impudence! I can't think why Macadam's taken that man up. (*crosses to fireplace. Enter* NINA, R.) Down at last, Nina?

NINA. Am I very late? I didn't get to sleep till half-past four. Who was that just went out? (*sits* R. *of table*)

TREV. Jenkyn, the *Glass of Fashion* man.

NINA. What did he want?*

TREV. He seemed to want me to show him the house.

NINA. What an idea! You didn't of course?

TREV. I showed him the door. (*sits* L. *of table*)

NINA.   Are these my letters ? Why, you **haven't** opened yours.

TREV.   I know what's inside without opening them.

NINA.   "A small and early at Mrs. Chetwynd's next Friday." What am I to wear ? I've positively nothing.

TREV.   Worth's bill !

NINA.   How much ?

TREV.   Three hundred pounds.

NINA.   That's very moderate. Oh, Norman !

TREV.   What, my dear ?

NINA.   A line from Mrs. Wedmore. She is going to Court at last——

TREV.   As petitioner, or——

NINA.   To be presented.

TREV.   Oh, I beg her pardon.

NINA.   (*opens another letter, which she hastily folds up and puts in her pocket. Slight pause. Opens another letter ;—reads*) "A card for Mrs. Goldney's *Tableaux Vivants !*"

TREV.   Another drop in Ionians. (*rises and goes back*)

NINA.   Have you any ?

TREV.   (*recovering himself*) A few, my dear, a few. And I told Harwood to sell out this morning.

NINA.   Let us hope he won't.

TREV.   I left him no option. They must be sold. I want the money.

NINA.   What is there so pressing ?

TREV.   (*comes down to* R. *of* NINA) Last week you asked me for one thousand pounds. You wouldn't tell me why. Still, I'm going to give it you.

NINA.   (*rises*) Oh, Norman, how good of you. **To**-day ? (*crosses to* R.)

Enter SERVANT, *with card on salver.*

SERV.   A gentleman to see you, sir.

TREV.   (*after reading card*) All right. (*turns to* NINA) From Harwood.

Exit SERVANT, L.

NINA.   (*to* TREVANION) You didn't answer me.

TREV.   I'll tell you when I've seen him. (*exit* L.)

NINA.   Just in time. (*takes letter from her pocket, and reads*)) "My dearest Nina,—I am so sorry to have to add to your anxieties just now, but you must tell your husband about the I. O. U., and ask him to let me have the money to-day. I have waited a week, and I really want it, or you know, my dear child, I wouldn't think of troubling you.—(*enter* PEG, R.) Yours most affectionately, Constance Coombe." (*sits* R. *of table*)

PEG. (*crosses to* NINA) What is the matter?

NINA. Read that! (*gives her letter, which* PEG. *reads*)

PEG. What does it mean?

NINA. Do you remember a paragraph in last week's *Glass* about a lady's losses at the card table?

PEG. Yes, what about it?

NINA. Do you know whom they meant? Me!

PEG. Nina, what have you done?

NINA. Only what all the rest did. I wish I'd never got into that set; but Norman was away, and I wanted excitement, distraction; and before I knew what I was doing I had lost heavily.

PEG. This is your secret. Why didn't you tell me before?

NINA. I was ashamed to confess how foolish I had been, even to myself.

PEG. How much do you owe?

NINA. I lost a thousand pounds.

PEG. Nina!

NINA. (*rising*) But I've paid half of it. (*crosses to* L.)

PEG. Where did you get the money?

NINA. Mr. Macadam lent it to me.

PEG. Did he know what for?

NINA. No; I only borrowed it till Norman's return, and every day I have been afraid that he might say something. That I. O. U. (*pointing to letter*) is for the rest.

PEG. You must tell Norman.

Re-enter SERVANT, L.

SERV. Prince Borowski!

NINA. Colonel Trevanion is engaged at present.

SERV. He said, might he see *you?*

PEG. What can he want?

NINA. Perhaps Lady Coombe has sent him. Show him in. (*exit* SERVANT, L.; NINA *takes* PEG *towards door*, R.)

PEG. Don't see him.

NINA. He may bring some message. I must see him.
Leave us for five minutes.

PEG. (*at door*) I hate Prince Borowski. (*exit*, R.)

Enter PRINCE BOROWSKI, L.

PRINCE. I am an early visitor this morning !

NINA. Very early ! You must excuse my husband.
He is engaged. (*crosses to sofa*)

PRINCE. Yes, so I ascertained. But it was to see you
madame, that I called. (NINA *sits on sofa*) You must
pardon me if I am indiscreet, but I know that Madame la
Comtesse has written to you, and I thought I might
perhaps, as a friend, be able to arrange this unfortunate
affair.

NINA. I have just received her letter.

PRINCE. Ah ! madame, if you would only confide in
me as the Comtesse does, perhaps I could be of service to
you. I have already contradicted the story of your embarrassments everywhere.

NINA. You are very good, Prince.

PRINCE. (*crosses to sofa*) Good, no ! It is the least
I can do (*sits on sofa*) to show the admiration I feel for
your noble character, your unfortunate position. Ah,
madame, when I think of it I cannot always be master of
my indignation.

NINA. What do you mean ?

PRINCE. That I know what the world suspects—that
you have been the victim of your faith in another. That
to-day your troubles and difficulties are caused because
that which is yours by right is kept from you. It is the
talk of the clubs.

NINA. (*turning to* PRINCE) Prince, you say you are
my friend. If you are sincere, tell me the worst. You
know what my husband has kept from me—tell me !

PRINCE. Perhaps I ought not. (*hesitating ; after a
look from* NINA) After all, it is better that you should
know it. It is said that he has gambled with your money.
That in one short year he has lost on the Stock Exchange
the whole of your fortune.

NINA. (*rising, and crossing to* L.) This, then, is the
mystery. Then this is the meaning of his grumbling at
my extravagance—of his wanting to live in the country.
(*pacing the room*) This is why he refuses me my own

and lets me be pressed on all sides for a few paltry hundreds. Oh, what a blind fool I have been! (*goes* L.)

PRINCE. (*crosses to* NINA) It distresses me to—to——

NINA. (*crosses to* PRINCE, C.) No, you have rendered me a great service, and I thank you for it. (*shakes hands*) I will see my husband again and come to an understanding.

PRINCE. You have already spoken to him?

NINA. But he has put me off. This explains the reason. He has loaded me with reproaches. Now the tables are turned.

PRINCE. It grieves me to have caused you this pain, but it is right you should know. To relieve you from your trouble your husband may not be able. His embarrassment is well known. But you may have other friends.

NINA. None, none of whom I could ask such a favor.

PRINCE. Do not say that. We have a saying in our country, if you cannot get over a mountain you can get round it. Madame, I might perhaps be your guide round that mountain which seems so great.

NINA. Prince, I thank you. You have always been a good friend to me.

PRINCE. Once I hoped that I might have been something more. (NINA *starts*) Ah, do not turn from me, madame. There is no wrong to you in what I say. It is of the past that I am thinking.

NINA. You must remember, Prince, then I was Nina O'Reilly—now I am Mrs. Trevanion. The past is dead!

PRINCE. And forgotten—the dead are always forgotten quickly. But it is in the name of friendship, madame, that I now say to you, if you are in trouble let me help you.

NINA. Thank you, but I will see my husband.

PRINCE. And if he cannot aid you?

Re-enter PEG *with basket of flowers*, R.

Remember I shall be at my studio at three.

PEG. Well, Prince?

PRINCE. Good-morning, Miss O'Reilly.

PEG. (R.) Don't let me disturb you.

PRINCE. (R. C.) I was just going. Good-morning,

mademoiselle. (*crosses to* NINA, L.) Au revoir, madame !

NINA. (L. C., *aside to him*) No, good-bye ! Whatever happens I must not come to you.

PRINCE. Whether you come or not I shall be there. (*exit, after a look at* NINA, L.)

PEG. Well, what does he want ?

NINA. Nothing !

PEG. Oh, Nina !

NINA. You are mistaken in the Prince, Peg. He is a true friend.

PEG. Why will he be at his studio at three ?

NINA. In case I should require his assistance. (*goes to table*, L.)

PEG. If you want assistance or advice there is only one man of whom you have the right to ask it—only one man who has the right to give it—your husband ! If the Prince Borowski offers you his counsel, believe me, Nina, it is not as your friend, but as your enemy.

NINA. Peg, I won't hear a word against the Prince. He has behaved most kindly.

PEG. Oh, how blind you are ! Cannot you understand his motives ; cannot you see the trap he's laid for you ?

NINA. What nonsense, Peg !

PEG. (*crosses to* NINA) Promise me, whatever happens, that——

NINA. I will make no promise. (*sits* R. C. ; *re-enter* TREVANION, L. ; *crosses to* TREVANION) Have you the money ?

TREV. I can give you half of it now. I'll **write a** cheque at once. (*sits and writes*)

NINA. (R. C.) Thank you so much. (*gets* R.)

Re-enter MACADAM, L.

MAC. (L. C.) Well, girls, how do you do ? Fine weather for the Flower Show. But where's my wife ? I expected to find her here.

NINA. Is she in town ?

MAC. Yes, my dear. Horace sneezed last night and she has come up to consult Sir William Jones. Didn't get home till five o'clock this morning ; out again at ten. Wonderful woman. It was a lucky day for me, the day I picked her up. (NINA *sits on sofa ;* PEG *arranges flowers*)

TREV. I am glad your marriage has turned out so happily.

MAC. (*going up to* TREVANION) Well, my dear boy —all is not gold that glitters. As regards happiness, between ourselves, a brewer who marries a countess is— small beer, very small beer.

TREV. You married Lady Coombe with your eyes open.

MAC. And Lady Coombe has opened 'em much wider since. But there, I don't complain ; I married a coat of arms, and I must pay for it.

TREV. You have what you bargained for. You wear the coat——

MAC. And she wears the breeches. (*comes down,* C.) By Jove, I got more than I bargained for this week.

TREV. Been buying something ?

MAC. No, it was rather a sell.

PEG. Another Vandyke ?

MAC. Not this time, my dear. I can't tell you exactly what it is—it is to be kept dark for the present. Talk about bargains, my dear, even the Läocoon's not in it. It's a big thing. (TREVANION *comes down to sofa*)

PEG. It must be big if it's bigger than that.

MAC. Oh, by-the-bye, Trevanion, you've got your cheque-book out ; I came away in such a fluster to-day I left mine at home. Could you oblige me with a cheque for a couple of hundreds ? I'll send you mine this afternoon. I've got a little matter to square up.

TREV. Another bargain ? (*sits again*)

MAC. Yes, a deuced bad one, too, this time. By the way, if you make it five, that'll settle what I lent Nina whilst you were away.

TREV. Lent Nina ? (*at table,* L.)

MAC. Hasn't she told you ?

NINA. (*in great agitation*) Yes, Norman, of course. This is partly what I wanted the money for. (TREVANION *looks at* NINA)

TREV. Thank you, Macadam. Thank you very much. (*with his eyes fixed on* NINA)

MAC. Don't mention it, dear boy, I was only too glad.

TREV. (*fetching cheque*) Here is the cheque all ready for you. (*gives it to* MACADAM)

MAC. Thanks! Now I'll go and look for Lady Coombe. Ta! ta! don't ring!

PEG. I'll go with you. (*looks across to* NINA; *to* MACADAM, *going* L.) Now, Mr. Macadam, what is it you've been buying?

MAC. Well, it's a secret just at present.

PEG. Something cheap, of course.

MAC. Dirt ch——(*looks at cheque, stops*) Well, I don't know; all things considered, I'm not so sure that it is. (*exit with* PEG, L. TREVANION *comes down*, C.; *pause*)

TREV. (L.) Why did you make this mystery? I thought you had everything you wanted; but if not, you might have told me so.

NINA. (R.) You were away.

TREV. But you might have written. Why did you go to Mr. Macadam?

NINA. (*rises and crosses to* L.) Would you have had me go to anybody else?

TREV. Nina, since we have been married, have I ever denied you anything? You have had your own way like the spoilt child that you are. I am in difficulties now through your extravagance. And then not to confide in me, to leave me to find out almost by accident who your creditor was! But you asked me for a thousand. Who is your creditor for the rest?

NINA. I shall not say. I have a right to spend what belongs to me. I don't ask you what you do with it. I have trusted implicitly to your honor, and what is the consequence? Within a year of our marriage you refuse me this paltry sum. (*crosses to fireplace*)

TREV. (*crosses to table* L.) Is there no other side to the picture? I give into your keeping my honor, my happiness. The young girl I married has developed into a giddy creature of fashion. For months the breach between us has been widening—the world becoming more and more to you, your home less and less.

NINA. If you have seen all this, why not have spoken before? (*crosses to* TREVANION, R. C.)

TREV. Because I wanted your own sense to speak for me and your own love to bring you back to me. Because I know when bitter words have once passed between man and wife, the words may be forgotten, but the freshness of their love is gone for ever. (*crosses to* R.)

NINA. (*at table* L.; *goes and sits* R. *of table*) Then why do you speak now ?

TREV. (R.) Because you have gone far enough, and you shall go no farther. I will no longer be the husband of Mrs. Trevanion, you shall be Colonel Trevanion's wife. I trusted you and I have been disappointed. (*sits sofa*)

NINA. Disappointed, and why ? Because you thought you were marrying a girl who knew nothing of the world, who would be content (*rises*) to be your housekeeper.

TREV. You are cruel, Nina. Some day you will bitterly repent.

NINA. I repent now. I repent that I allowed myself to be the blind dupe I was—I who might have done so differently.

TREV. What do you mean ?

NINA. Oh you men, you men ! You put a ring upon a woman's finger, and from that moment you think her will is to be yours, her life, her liberty, her happiness are to be your property. (*sits* R. *of table*) Norman, will you do as I ask ?

TREV. Once for all—no ! (*rises and goes back*)

Re-enter PEG, L., *comes down* L. *of table.*

PEG. What's that ?

NINA. Only my ring. (*toying with wedding-ring*)

PEG. Oh, it's so unlucky to take off your wedding-ring.

NINA. Mine comes off by itself.

PEG. That's worse.

NINA. It's all been a mistake from the first.

TREV. (*comes down* R. *of* NINA ; PEG *gets back*) Will you think where you would like to spend the remainder of the season ?

NINA. (*rises*) I shall not leave London. Why is it you are anxious to keep me from all society ? Because you have something you wish to conceal from me. Because I ask inconvenient questions. Because you have found out I am no longer the blind hasty girl you married. I will no longer be put off with excuses. What is this mystery about my fortune ?

TREV. I cannot tell you. (*crosses to* L.)

NINA. (*crosses to* TREVANION) Then I will tell *you*. You have been gambling. You have used it to pay your losses.

3

PEG. Nina ! (C., *at back*)

NINA. I have it upon good authority.

TREV. You have been told so !

NINA. Yes, and I believe it.

TREV. (*crosses to* NINA, C.) Who is **my** accuser ?

NINA, You have your secret ; that is mine. (*goes* R.)

TREV. (*getting between* NINA *and door*, R.) Where are you going ?

NINA. In future where I choose. I have my own rank in society. You married me for my fortune, and you have enjoyed it, but your authority is at an end. You shall dictate to me no longer,—to me, who might have been a princess.

TREV. Ah, you have betrayed your secret.

NINA. (*to* PEG, *who intercepts her*) Let me go. (*flings her aside ; exit,* R.)

TREV. (*sits* R. *of* L. *table*) Borowski !

Re-enter SERVANT, L.

SERV. Lady Coombe.

Enter LADY COOMBE, *with poodle*, L. TREVANION *rises.*

LADY C. Ah, my dear ! good-morning. Would you hold Horace ? Thanks. (*gives poodle to* SERVANT, *who exits*, L.) How are you, dear ? You must excuse me coming upstairs, but I thought my husband——

PEG. Mr. Macadam has been gone some time.

LADY C. Dear me, how provoking ! I wanted him particularly. How is Nina ?

TREV. Peg, tell your sister Lady Coombe is here. Won't you sit down ? (*points to sofa*)

LADY C. Quite well, I hope. These east winds are so trying. (*exit* PEG, R.) You will be grieved to hear Horace is quite an invalid. (*sits on sofa ; crosses to* R. *and sits*)

TREV. (*crosses to* LADY COOMBE) I don't think Nina will be very long.

LADY C. To tell the truth, it is you, Colonel, I have called to see. I daresay you have guessed my errand.

TREV. Not at all.

LADY C. I must apologize for my delay in coming, but what with my engagements this last week and Horace's precarious condition, I've really had no time to think of money matters.

TREV. Money?

LADY C. At last, however, I have brought the memorandum. (*produces I. O. U. gives it to* TREVANION)

TREV. An I. O. U. of Nina's?

LADY C. (*rises*) Have I done wrong?

TREV. Five hundred pounds?

LADY C. Surely you knew——

TREV. She may have mentioned it. I had forgotten
it. (*controls himself with effort*)

LADY C. Poor child, she has been most unfortunate.
You can't think how distressed I was to find the papers
had got hold of it.

TREV. Papers!

LADY C. The paragraph is copied everywhere.

TREV. What paragraph?

LADY C. In last week's *Glass*. The lady well-known
in society——

TREV. Is Nina?

LADY C. Surely she has told you.

TREV. My wife has lost this money at play?

LADY C. I am afraid I have been indiscreet. (TRE-
VANION *gaze at I. O. U.—slight pause*)

TREV. Does anybody know it is my wife?

LADY C. I don't think so, except the Prince.

TREV. Borowski knows it? Perhaps he is the author
of the paragraph.

LADY C. Oh, the Prince is discretion itself. He
would tell nobody; and when you have redeemed the
I. O. U., the matter ends.

TREV. Lady Coombe, I acknowledge Nina's signa-
ture, and it shall be redeemed this afternoon. (*returns
I. O. U.*)

LADY C. Thank you. I hope I haven't caused you
any annoyance, but really I thought it better for the dear
child's sake to let you know about it. It will be a load
off her mind, for she seemed to have some absurd scruple
about telling you herself.

TREV. I appreciate your kindness. (*shakes hands*)
And I thank you for the service you have rendered Nina
and myself. (*rings bell*)

Re-enter PEG, R.

PEG. Nina sends her love and asks you to excuse her,
she's dressing.

LADY C. Certainly, dear. I am not often out so early, but I have been with Horace to Sir William Jones. (*Re-enter* SERVANT, L., *with poodle, crosses to* LADY COOMBE) Poor dear! Sir William says he is far from strong. (*shakes hands with* PEG. *Exit* SERVANT, L.) Good-morning! (*exit,* L.)

PEG. (R.) Then she has told you?

TREV. (L. C.; *comes down* R. *of table*) Yes, that my wife is a gamester; that she has made her name and mine the sport of every club and drawing-room.

PEG. Nobody knows it yet.

TREV. Borowski know it. What she has hidden from me she has confided to that man. (*sits*)

Re-enter MACADAM *with paper*, L.

MAC. There you are, Trevanion. I was obliged to come and show you this. The second number of the *Glass*—just out. "Mr. John Macadam, of Fairmead." Two columns and a half! What do you think of that? Capital description of my place. Touching reference, dear boy, to yourself and that Rorke's Drift affair.

TREV. Macadam, (*rises*) you seem to know a great deal about this paper. Who puts in the paragraphs? (PEG *takes paper*)

MAC. From all I hear, the paragraphs get in by accident. But why do you ask me? (*crosses to* L.) My dear fellow, you seem upset. There hasn't been anything about you in it, has there?

TREV. No—but about Nina.

MAC. About my ward? (*aside*) I'll break that Jenkyn's head.

Enter TOM *with paper*, L.

TOM. I say, Peg, seen the *Glass*?

MACADAM *snatches paper away;* TOM *takes one from* PEG.

PEG. No, I don't want to.

MAC. No, don't want to—we don't want to. (*aside*) Damn it, there may be something else in it.

TOM. Oh, but here's another paragraph about sublime ignorance's wife.

TREV. What? (*snatches paper*)

MAC. (*aside*) Jenkyn again!

TREV. (*reads*) "Apropos of the lady whose losses at play formed the subject of a recent paragraph, there is no truth in the report that her mysterious visits to the studio of a distinguished foreign amateur will shortly be the subject of a judicial investigation."

> TOM *laughs during the reading ;* PEG *pulls him sharply round.* TREVANION *crumples paper up in his hands and crosses to door.*

PEG. Norman !

MAC. Where are you going ? (*music*)

TREV. To the office ! Come with me. I shall want a witness. This infamous paragraph is about my wife. (*exit*, L.)

TOM. Nina ?

MAC. Nina ? and in my society journal ? (*quick curtain*) Damn society journals ! (*tears up paper and jumps on it*)

END OF ACT II.

ACT III.

SCENE.—BOROWSKI'S *studio. Entrance* L., *and a small side door*, R. *At back*, C., *an inner room, separated by a curtain. Window* L. *at back ; an easel*, L. C., *with a baize thrown over it. Another similarly draped in a corner. Other easels, statuary, casts, etc., about.* PRINCE *enters through curtain*, C., *smoking a cigarette, an open letter in his hand.*

PRINCE. Thanks, mon cher compatriot, for the warning. So there have been inquiries about me at the Foreign Office ? It is fortunate that I have a friend at court. Shall I go or brave it out ? Shall I stay, while they know everywhere I have been an honored guest, that the Polish Prince is but an adventurer with a great talent for winning at play ? It is unfortunate, for never have I found dupes so simple as the English aristocrat. Your stock-in-trade a title, a foreign accent, and a suit of evening dress, and the doors of society are opened wide to you. Who can be making inquiries ? Who can suspect me ?

Of whom have I been winning lately ? Mrs. Trevanion ?
No ! La Comtesse ? No, she has not brains enough ;
besides, she is coming here to-day to pay me. No, it's
some one more dangerous. (*walks about, pacing studio*)

Enter SERVANT, L., *then* LADY COOMBE.

SERV. Lady Coombe. (*exit*, L.)

PRINCE. (*watch*) You are late, Madame la Comtesse. I had given you up.

LADY C. I have only just received the cheque from
Colonel Trevanion. I came to you at once. (*gives him
envelope*)

PRINCE. (*taking it*) Thanks ! I hope, madame,
you will be more fortunate another time.

LADY C. Prince, I shall never touch a card again.
What with my losses, Horace's illness—— (*sits*, R.)

PRINCE. *Ce cher Horace !* (*ready knock*, R.)

LADY C. Ah, those dreadful rumors !

PRINCE. (*starts ; aside*) What has she heard ?
(*aloud*) What rumors, madame ?

LADY C. Would you believe it ? They're saying now
that *I* am the lady whose husband is in sublime ignorance
of her embarrassments. What will they say next ?

PRINCE. (*sits* R. *of table*) It is hard to tell ! They
will end by saying what is true !

LADY C. But how has it got known ?

PRINCE. Probably it is only a surmise. But happily
it does not matter much.

LADY C. Not matter ! when my reputation is at stake !

PRINCE. You take too serious a view of it. Such a
report enhances rather than detracts from a lady's reputation.

LADY C. You evidently haven't seen the *Glass*.

PRINCE. Not the new number.

LADY C. Read that, Prince. (*points out paragraph*)

PRINCE. (*reads*) " Apropos of the lady whose losses
at play formed the subject of a recent paragraph, there is
no truth in the report that her mysterious visits to the
studio of a distinguished foreign amateur will shortly be
the subject of a judicial investigation. Beauty is sitting
for her portrait. *Voilà tout.*" (*rises*) Ah, I know nothing of this paragraph.

LADY C. You see, I am clearly indicated. I have lost
and I visit your studio.

PRINCE. Does not this rather show that neither paragraph applies to you?

LADY C. (*rises*) Look at the last line.—"Beauty is sitting for her portrait."

PRINCE. That is the line I was looking at.

LADY C. I have been sitting for my portrait. *Voilà tout.* (*sits*)

PRINCE. True! (*looks at watch*) But I am afraid I am detaining you. Do not disturb yourself. If anybody calls, it will only be Jenkyn.

LADY C. Oh that man! (*rises*) He mustn't see me here. It would confirm everything, and who knows what the *next paragraph would be!* (*a knock,* R.) Heavens, who is that?

PRINCE. Ah, it is his knock. (*opens door,* L.) You can go out this way. He has come *to the side door!* (*another knock,* R.; *shakes hands*) *À bientôt!* (*exit* LADY COOMBE, L. PRINCE *crosses to door,* R.) Jenkyn— I must get rid of him. Mrs. Trevanion may be here. (*opens door,* R.)

Enter MACADAM, *dragging in* JENKYN.

Ah, Mr. Macadam!

JEN. Leave go, sir. I will not be dragged into a room like this.

MAC. Dragged into a room! What have you dragged me into?

PRINCE. (*comes down* C.) What is the matter, gentlemen?

MAC. (L.) The matter! Why, the matter is the *Glass of Fashion!*

JEN. (R.) Upon my soul, I don't know how it got in! When I saw it, you could have knocked me down with a feather.

MAC. I could ha' knocked you down without one, when I saw it!

PRINCE. Saw what?

MAC. Oh, I suppose you're like Jenkyn. *You* haven't seen it. It's infamous. Six actions on my hands already, and this is the last straw. (*sits* L. *of* R. *table*)

PRINCE. On your hands. Ah, then you are the new proprietor.

MAC. Worse luck.

PRINCE. (L. C.) You have a fine property.

JEN.   A very fine property.

MAC.   Property be hanged !   I'm losing money every day by the *Glass !*

JEN.   Well, you're making it by the barrel.

MAC.   I wouldn't mind the loss, but fancy in my own paper my best friends held up to ridicule, my own ward insulted.   (*rises*)   I suppose there'll be a paragraph about my wife next, and then you'll wonder how the devil *that* got in !   (*crosses to* L.)

JEN.   My dear sir——

MAC.   Damme !   I wonder you don't libel *me*, say I get drunk.   Egad !   I *have* taken a *Glass* too much. (*gets* R.)

PRINCE.   (*comes down between them*)   Gentlemen, let me remind you this is not the office of your paper.   What have I to do with your private quarrels ?

MAC.   What have you to do with them ?   There's been a most disgraceful paragraph about the visits of a lady to your studio.   Where is it ?   Here !   (*pulls out papers*) No, that's a writ—that's a summons—I can't find the thing, but it's about my ward, and that's enough for me.

PRINCE.   Your ward ?   Ah, it is about Mrs. Trevanion !   Mr. Jenkyn, you have been so indiscreet as to print such a thing ?

MAC.   Oh, bless you, he don't know anything about it, It dropped down the chimney.   (*goes up*)

JEN.   (*aside to* PRINCE)   I say, you must pull me through.   Colonel Trevanion's been to the office, and I was obliged to say where I got my information.

PRINCE.   What information ?

JEN.   Didn't you tell me Mrs. Trevanion had been sitting for our series ?

PRINCE.   It is not true !

MAC.   (*coming down to back of table*)   There ! there you are !   What did I tell you ?

PRINCE.   Jenkyn, dear child, you're a fool.

Enter SERVANT, *who speaks aside to* PRINCE.

JEN.   I beg your pardon.

MAC.   There, you can beg *his* pardon.   Why don't you beg Colonel Trevanion's ?   Now you can contradict it on the Prince's authority.

JEN.   (R.)   Or justify it.

MAC. (C.) Justify it! What do you mean? You know there isn't a word of truth in it.

JEN. That's what was said in the paragraph.

MAC. (*crosses to* R.) I wash my hands of the whole affair. Jenkyn, you can look out for another shop.

JEN. That's the fourth time you have given me notice. I shall take it presently.

MAC. I'll have an editor who knows less about other people's business and more about his own.

JEN. Oh, then I hope you'll find one.

MAC. They're to be picked up cheap enough, dirt cheap.

PRINCE. (*who has meanwhile dismissed* SERVANT, *crosses to door*) Gentlemen, I'm very sorry I have not another room to offer you, and I have to keep an appointment here. Good-morning. (*opens door*, R.)

MAC. Come along! You come round to Sloane Street at once, and apologize.

JEN. Look here. They don't know you're the proprietor. Why are you in such a state of mind about it?

MAC. I introduced you to the house and they look upon you as my friend.

JEN. But if I'm discharged, I needn't apologize. You can do it yourself. (*goes to door*, R.)

MAC. If Trevanion knew I had anything to do with the *Glass*, I could never look him in the face again.

JEN. Prince, I——

MACADAM, *who is at door*, R., *seizes* JENKYN *and drags him off*, R ; PRINCE *locks door*, R. *Enter* NINA, L.

PRINCE. (*crosses to her*) Welcome, madame! (R.)

NINA. I am rather early. (*shakes hands*, L.)

PRINCE. Mrs. Trevanion cannot come too soon.

NINA. Did you expect me?

PRINCE. I am not surprised. Of course, it is in my quality of artist that you honor me with this visit.

NINA. Of course. I have come to sit to you.

PRINCE. Your husband has withdrawn his objection.

NINA. Prince, I please myself.

PRINCE. (R. C.) And you please me. Will you be so kind as to sit there? (NINA *sits* R. *of table*) Now, a pensive attitude—the eyes cast down and an expression of fixed melancholy—the hand so. Will you not take off your glove, that I may sketch the hand? (NINA *takes off*

left glove ; he takes it and lays it on table at back)   Ah,
your monogram ! How pretty !

NINA.   I worked it myself ! (PRINCE *stands looking
at her*) Will that do ?

PRINCE.   I am not satisfied with the expression.

NINA.   You are hard to please. (*smiles*)

PRINCE.   That smile is perfect, but not what I want.
A gentle melancholy—an air of resignation. Think—
think of your husband. (*begins to sketch*)

NINA.   Ah ! (*sighs*) I am afraid there is some truth
in what you said. There is some mystery about my
property.

PRINCE.   It is a painful thing to sow dissension between
husband and wife, but I could not stand by and see you
wronged.

NINA.   Now, what is to be done ? This I. O. U. must
be met somehow.

PRINCE.   Do not disturb yourself, madame. It has
been paid.

NINA.   Paid ! By whom ?

PRINCE.   Madame, that is a secret. Lady Coombe has
her money.

NINA.   And the memorandum ?

PRINCE.   You need distress yourself no more about it.

NINA.   How can I thank you ? I will not remain
your debtor long.

PRINCE.   (*aside*) She thinks *I* have paid it. (*aloud*)
Hélas, madame, to-morrow I shall bid you good-bye,
perhaps for ever.

NINA.   You're going away, Prince ?

PRINCE.   Yes, madame. Political reasons. Amongst
the friends I have made in England there is one I shall
regret above all others—yourself !

NINA.   (*rising*) I must go now.

PRINCE.   Pardon—the sketch is not finished—and yet
it might be recognized already. Won't you look at it ?
(*turns easel to audience*)

NINA.   (*crosses and looks*) It is very good !

PRINCE.   (*sighing*) But, hélas, how unworthy the
original ! (*covers sketch*)

NINA.   On the contrary, I am afraid it is too flattering.

PRINCE.   It is not the hand of the artist that has repro-
duced Mrs. Trevanion. (*crosses to* NINA) It is the
heart of the man.

NINA. You are a poet as well as a painter, Prince.

PRINCE. Mrs. Trevanion! (*passionately*) Nina! (NINA *starts back*) It is neither the poet nor the painter who speaks to you now. It is the lover. (*seizes her hand*)

NINA. Hush, Prince, hush! I must not—will not hear this.

PRINCE. Love is a passion beyond our control. To-day, alone with you here, my secret leaps from my heart to my lips. Nina, I love you.

NINA. Let me go. This is cowardly.

PRINCE. Directly our eyes met I knew you were my fate, and ever since then I have been wrestling with my destiny. But it is too strong for me—and too strong for you.

NINA. I am stronger than you think. (*breaks away to L. door ; crosses R.; then rushes to L.*)

PRINCE. (*intercepting her*) You shall not go! When you promised to come here——

NINA. I didn't know you would insult me.

PRINCE. (L. C.) Love is not an insult.

NINA. This is not love !

PRINCE. (L.) Call it by what name you choose, you have no right to be indignant. ; A thousand times you have encouraged me to speak, and now that I have spoken you reproach me.

NINA. It is false ; let me pass. (PRINCE *intercepts her*)

PRINCE. No !

NINA. Take care, Prince ; you forget I have a husband.

PRINCE. Nay, it is you who have forgotten that.

NINA. What have I done ?

PRINCE. More than you know. You have not seen this. (*shows paragraph in the journal*) Your visits here are common talk.

NINA. Coward ! This is your work.

PRINCE. If you are found here, what will people say ?

NINA. No one shall find me.

PRINCE. I expect some friends. (NINA *tries to pass*) You cannot go except with my consent. (NINA *makes a dash at door*, R., *but finds it locked*)

NINA. Locked ! This is a plot. (*sinks on chair*, R.)

PRINCE. (*approaches her*) But do not be distressed.

One word and you are free. (*bends over her*) Will you not speak it? (NINA *rises suddenly as if to strike him*) Ah! *Re-enter* SERVANT, L.) I am at home. (*exit*, SERVANT, L.)

NINA. (R.) Some one is coming. (*rises*)

PRINCE. See! (L. C.; *draws back curtain*, C., *showing the inner room*) I give you one more chance. (NINA *runs out*, C. L.; PRINCE *draws curtain*. *Enter* PEG, L.; *aside*) Peste! (*advancing*) Miss O'Reilly? (R.)

PEG. (*coming down*, L.) Yes, Prince, Miss O'Reilly!

PRINCE. That is indeed an honor!

PEG. I've come to have my portrait taken!

PRINCE. How unfortunate! If I had known that you were coming, I should not——

PEG. Have been at home? (*crosses to* R.)

PRINCE. On the contrary, I would have kept myself at liberty.

PEG. Are you so busy? (*goes up back*)

PRINCE. I regret to say that I have an appointment. (*goes up back*)

PEG. Yes, I know.

PRINCE. You know?

PEG. With my sister. That's why I came.

PRINCE. Mrs. Trevanion has not yet arrived.

PEG. I'll wait for her. (*coming down* R.)

PRINCE. (*dismayed*) Wait for her?

PEG. When the sketch is finished, we can go home together.

PRINCE. But it will take some time. You will be tired.

PEG. I can sit down. (*sits* R. *of table*)

PRINCE. But, Miss O'Reilly—do not think me rude, I am expecting other visitors.

PEG. Indeed! We shall be quite a party.

PRINCE. (*aside*) Damn! What shall I do?

PEG. It's strange that Nina isn't here yet.

PRINCE. Ladies are not punctual.

PEG. She left home more than half an hour ago. (*seeing easel*) You've been sketching somebody? (*crosses to easel*, L.)

PRINCE. Excuse me, this is an unfinished sketch. (R.)

PEG. What a queer place this is! (*approaching curtain*, C.) Where does that lead to?

PRINCE. (*intercepting her*) That is my room.

PEG. Oh! (*goes* R.) Here's another door.

PRINCE. (*crosses and unlocks door*) You can go out into the street that way.

PEG. (*looks outside*) Thank you! (*goes and sits* R. PRINCE *puts himself between* PEG *and the easel* L., *throwing his arm over the baize*) I wonder whether Nina will be long. It is too bad of her to keep you waiting.

PRINCE. Oh, I can always occupy myself, and just now I am busier than usual.

PEG. Perhaps I am interrupting you?

PRINCE. To tell the truth—you will excuse me speaking plainly?

PEG. By all means.

PRINCE. I have no time to spare.

PEG. (*rises*) You want me to go?

PRINCE. Excuse my bluntness.

PEG. Certainly! Excuse mine! I'm not going. (*sits*, R.)

PRINCE. Not going?

PEG. Without my sister.

PRINCE. I will be frank with you. Mrs. Trevanion is coming here on business.

PEG. Mrs. Trevanion has no business here.

PRINCE. (*sits*) I think I understand you!

PEG. Then we understand each other.

PRINCE. The matron used to chaperon the maid; but to-day, it is the maid who chaperons the matron.

PEG. It is the matron who needs chaperoning.

PRINCE. You mistrust your sister?

PEG. No! I mistrust *you!*

PRINCE. (*rises*) We are becoming very frank indeed.

PEG. Your studio is not a fit place for her.

PRINCE. A studio not a fit place for a lady?

PEG. I said *your* studio.

PRINCE. Perhaps you are right! (*gets at back of table*) My studio is not a fit place for some ladies. *Par exemple*, if you were found here alone, it might be awkward to explain your presence. (*re-enter* SERVANT, L.; *crosses to* SERVANT, L.) Some one is here. Show him up. (*exit* SERVANT, L.; PEG *rises*) It is a gentleman. (*comes* C. *to* PEG, *standing between her and the curtain with his back to it*)

PEG. (*with her face to* PRINCE *and curtain*) It is my sister.

PRINCE. On my word of honor! No! (NINA *looks through curtain* C.)

PEG. (*seeing her utters a cry; then quickly*) He is coming; give me time to go!

PRINCE. Quick! I will keep him back!

> *Points to door*, R., *and exits*, L. *Whilst* PRINCE *exits*, PEG *points to door*, R. *exit* NINA, R. *Exit* PEG, C. *All this as quick as possible. No pause.*

Re-enter PRINCE, L.

PRINCE. (*smiling*) Gone! (*turns*, L.) Walk in, Mr. Stanhope.

Enter TOM, L.

TOM. (*looking about*) Humph! rather a neat crib you have here.

PRINCE. Yes—it has its conveniences! (*listens a moment at the curtain*)

TOM. Where's Peg?

PRINCE. Ah, you expected to meet Miss O'Reilly?

TOM. She said last night she should be here at three. Hasn't she come yet?

PRINCE. She has come and gone.

TOM. Hang it all, she might have waited for a fellow. How's she come out? Let's look! (*approaches easel*)

PRINCE. I have not yet sketched Miss O'Reilly. I had another appointment.

TOM. Then who is this?

PRINCE. Another lady.

TOM. Oh—I know! the lady mentioned in the *Glass?*

PRINCE. Yes!

TOM. Let's look! (*throws aside baize*)

PRINCE. Pardon! (*too late to stop him*)

TOM. Nina!

PRINCE. Chut! she might hear you. (*points to curtain*)

TOM. She is there?

Re-enter SERVANT, L.

SERV. Colonel Trevanion!

TOM. Norman!

PRINCE. (*covers portrait*) I will come down. (*crosses* L. *Exeunt* SERVANT *and* PRINCE, L.)

TOM. If Norman saw the portrait ! (*looks about, sees easel in corner, exchanges the two portraits*)

Re-enter PRINCE, L., *followed by* TREVANION.

PRINCE. (C.) This way, Colonel !

TREV. (L.) You here, Stanhope ?

PRINCE. I could wish that my little works of art were worthier of your examination.

TREV. I haven't come to criticise, but to demand an explanation.

PRINCE. If there is anything I can explain——

TREV. (*shows* PRINCE *a copy of the journal*) This paragraph !

PRINCE. I have seen that.

TREV. Then you will understand the object of my visit ?

PRINCE. Not at all.

TREV. This I am told is the studio, and my wife is the lady.

PRINCE. Impossible !

TREV. The editor himself has admitted it.

PRINCE. I cannot hold myself responsible for the insinuations of the journals of society.

TREV. He has given *you* as his authority. I forbade my wife to sit to you. Has she done so ?

PRINCE. My appointment was with another lady. No, a mistake has been made. It was Miss O'Reilly I arranged to sketch.

TREV. Peg !

TOM. That's why *I'm* here. She told me she was coming.

PRINCE. How fortunate I have corroboration !

TREV. If Mr. Jenkyn has misunderstood you, he owes *you* an apology as well as me. Will you come with me to him ?

PRINCE. I regret to say, some friends are coming to look round my studio.

TREV. I will not leave the matter as it stands. (*knock and ring*, L. ; *crosses to* L.)

PRINCE. There they are ! I must ask you to excuse me.

TREV.   I will wait here until your friends have gone. (*goes up to curtain*, C.)

TOM.   (*intercepting him on one side*) Someone is there.

PRINCE.   (*intercepting him on the other*)   A lady!

TREV.   You've a great many visitors. (*crosses to* R.)

PRINCE.   It is the series I am sketching for the *Glass*.

Re-enter MACADAM, LADY COOMBE *and* JENKYN, L.

MAC.   Oh, there you are, Trevanion—(*crosses to* R.)— we've just come from Sloane Street. Apologize! (*gets to back*)

TREV.   (*to* JENKYN) Mr. Jenkyn, the Prince says you have misunderstood him.

JEN.   Not at all.

MAC.   (*aside to* JENKYN) Apologize!

PRINCE.   (*comes down* C.) I said nothing to you about Mrs. Trevanion. I did not mention names.

JEN.   *I* didn't mention names.

PRINCE.   It is not true that she has been here.

JEN.   I *said* it wasn't true.

MAC.   (*aside to* JENKYN) Will you apologize?

JEN.   If I had said it *was* true, I could have understood your indignation; but when I say it *isn't* true——

TREV.   You hint the lie you are afraid to write.

JEN.   Really, I have nothing to retract.

TREV.   But I shall make you.

MAC.   (*aside*) There! I knew he would!

TREV.   I don't mean you, but your proprietor.

MAC.   Phew! (*turns up*)

TREV.   The guilt is his who makes a profit out of this garbage. (*flings paper down*)

MAC.   (L. C., *coming down*) There isn't a profit— there's a loss.

LADY C.   (L.) How do *you* know?

MAC.   I've heard so. (*goes up with* LADY COOMBE)

JEN.   You are excited, Colonel. You forget, the Press has certain privileges.

TREV.   *You* are not the Press. You have no more share in its dignity than it has in your impudence.

JEN.   (*stepping forward*) Impudence! Take care, Colonel Trevanion; you will force me to justify——

MAC.   Egad! He wants the Colonel to apologize to *him!*

JEN. (*looking at easel significantly*) Some one has been here to-day.

PRINCE. It was another lady—whom I have been sketching. (*comes down* C.)

TREV. Is that the lady in that room ? (*going up* R.)

JEN. A lady in that room ! Perhaps that is your wife.

TREV. My wife ! (*rushes up, draws curtain back.* PEG *discovered reading in other room.* PRINCE *rushes up after* TREVANION.

TOM. Peg !

JEN. *and* LADY C. Miss O'Reilly !

PEG. (*rises and comes down*) Ready, Prince ?

TREV. (*comes down to table*) Now, Mr. Jenkyn, what have you to say ?

MAC. He apologizes ! He apologizes ! (*music commences pianissimo, then swell*)

JEN. Oh, it's Miss O'Reilly you've been sketching ? *lays hold of baize*) This, then, is the mysterious lady ! (*throws off baize*) Lady Coombe ! (LADY COOMBE *screams and falls into arm-chair*, L.)

ALL. Lady Coombe !

MAC. My wife !

> *Quick curtain.* MACADAM *falls into chair* L. *of table.* TREVANION'S *hand falls on the glove which lies on the table. He takes it up and sees the monogram.*

END OF ACT III.

ACT IV.

SCENE.—*Same at Act II.*

PEG *discovered looking at bracelet.*

PEG. Oh, what a dear, darling, delightful birthday present ! Tom *has* good taste. Of course he has, or he wouldn't have fallen in love with *me*. (*sits sofa*) Norman hasn't given me a present yet, and he always does. Fancy me twenty-one to-day. I'm not a minor now - (*rises*)—I'm a major—Major Peg O'Reilly. Oh dear me, I should feel so happy if Nina and Norman were only friends again. It seems wicked of me to have a birthday while they are so miserable. (*crosses to* L.)

Enter TREVANION, R.

(*crosses to* TREVANION, C.) Oh, Norman! look what Tom's sent me! isn't it a beautiful present? Poor dear, he must have gone without a lot of cigars for it.

TREV. Peg, you seem very fond of Tom. (*bracelet on*)

PEG. I wouldn't change my Tom for anyone.

TREV. He's very poor.

PEG. So am I —we're a good match.

TREV. Tell me, if you had been an heiress and so rich you might have married anyone, should you have chosen him?

PEG. Yes, out of all the world.

TREV. Tom is a lucky fellow. (*crosses to chair* R. *of table*)

PEG. And he knows it.

TREV. Luckier than he thinks. (*sits* R. *of table*)

PEG. Whatever do you mean? (*comes up to him*)

TREV. Peg, you're of age to-day. To-day I have to tell you something which should have been told you long ago but for the sacred promise I had given. You know I was your father's brother officer and friend?

PEG. Poor father!

TREV. He made me the confidant of a secret which affected the future of two young girls. The one is now my wife, the other is yourself.

PEG. Oh, Norman dear, I wish you would come to the point. I always read the third volume first.

TREV. But I must commence with the first volume of this story. It began when your father and mother met. In the first volume, Nina, your sister, was born. In the second, her parents were married.

PEG. (*realizing his meaning*) Norman! (*drops away*)

TREV. (*rises*) They could not marry before. There were legal difficulties in the way. The third volume began with your birth. To-day we reach the last chapter. Law is not a thing many women understand, but you have heard enough of it to know that you are the only daughter the law recognizes. The third volume, Peg, gives you the O'Reilly estates.

PEG. And Nina? (*looking up to* TREVANION)

TREV. Is married to a man who wooed her knowing

that she would only bring him her beauty—and—he thought—her love.

PEG. (*crosses to table*) My poor sister! Oh, Norman! She never knew this!

TREV. No, it was to be kept from you both as long as possible.

PEG. This explains the mystery that has led to all our unhappiness! How cruelly you have been misjudged!

TREV. If that were all, I could forgive her. The charge she brought against me was made in anger, and she has withdrawn it.

PEG. What more can she do?

TREV. (*comes forward to* L. *of table*) Nina was at Borowski's yesterday. You deceived everybody except me!

PEG. Norman!

TREV. (*producing glove*) I found this on a table in the studio.

PEG. (*turns away*) Her glove! (*going to door*, R.)

TREV. Where are you going? (*follows her*)

PEG. To tell her.

TREV. No, don't tell her anything. You kept her secret from *me*, (*crosses to* PEG) and you must keep mine from *her*. Promise.

PEG. But why, Norman?

TREV. I have still faith enough in her to hope she will tell me herself.

Enter MACADAM, L. ; *comes down*, C.

MAC. Bless you, my dear, how are you? (*business.* PEG *goes to door*, R.)

TREV. Peg knows everything.

PEG. (*at door*) Don't speak to me. I can hardly realize it. I must go and think it out all by myself. Poor Nina! (*exit*, R.)

MAC. (*sits sofa*) My dear fellow, I am glad you've told her. I was afraid you'd want *me* to, and I'm so worried, what with one thing and another, I should only ha' made a hash of it. What does Nina say?

TREV. I haven't told her yet.

MAC. It'll be an awful blow to her. But I've had nothing but blows lately, and on the top of it comes this ridiculous nonsense about my wife and Borowski. It's too preposterous. The worst of it is, she thinks *she's* the beauty referred to in the *Glass*, and wants me to go to law about it. (*aside*) Gad, I should look well bringing an action against myself.

TREV.   I can quite sympathize with Lady Coombe. I'm in much the same position.

MAC.   It was proved yesterday that Nina wasn't meant, but my wife *had* been sitting for her portrait ; though how anything she saw in the *glass* could convince her she was a beauty, I can't think.

TREV.   You don't believe there was any foundation for the paragraph ?

MAC.   My dear fellow, it's an infamous concoction of that scoundrel, Jenkyn.

TREV.   One part of it is true, at any rate.   The husband of the lady referred to *is* about to take judicial proceedings.

MAC.   Against the wife ?

TREV.   No, against the proprietor.

MAC.   (*rising and crossing to* TREVANION)   The proprietor !   My dear fellow, he's nothing to do with it.   I daresay he's as much annoyed as you are.   (*aside*)   I know he is.

TREV.   He is the responsible person.

MAC.   Now, if you pitched into the editor !

TREV.   A man of straw !

MAC.   The printer ?

TREV.   A mere workman.   No, Macadam—(*rises, lays his hand on* MACADAM'S *shoulder*)—the owner is the chief offender.

MAC.   Phew !

TREV.   It's no use appealing to his sense of honor.

MAC.   Why ?

TREV.   Such a man hasn't any.

MAC.   What are you going to do ?

TREV.   To instruct my solicitor to prosecute.   (*looks at watch*)   If I go now, I shall just catch him.   (*goes to door,* L.)

MAC.   (*following him*)   My dear boy, think of what you're about.   The poor devil might be sent to the Old Bailey.   Do you know who he is ?

TREV.   No ; the paper's changed hands.   The new owner's not been registered, but we shall ascertain to-day——

MAC.   Trevanion, my dear boy, I'll confess.

TREVANION *shuts door after him. Exit, L.*

(*comes down*) Hang it, I daren't tell him. Here's a pretty kettle of fish. This is ruling the social and political world, and having society at my feet. I know what I shall have at my feet before long—this sort of thing. (*imitates working treadmill*) The day I'm tried at the Old Bailey, there'll be an offensive paragraph about the judge, and Jenkyn'll wonder how on earth that got in. I can't brazen it out. I shall have to emigrate. I can't look 'em in the face when they all know it. Jones, Mrs. Nemo, Nina, my own ward, Trevanion, my dearest friend, my wife—Jenkyn has libelled the lot. I know what the end of it will be. My portrait'll be in the *Police News* next week. Jenkyn'll know how *that* got in. (*goes up, L.*)

Re-enter PEG, R.

PEG.   Are you going, Mr. Macadam ?

MAC.   Yes, my dear, to Timbuctoo.

PEG.   Good gracious !

MAC.   I shall be back directly. (*exit, L.*)

PEG.   (*goes up, looking after* MACADAM) Whatever can be the matter with Mr. Macadam ?

Enter NINA, R.

NINA.   (*looking about the room*) Peg !

PEG.   (*turns*) What are you looking for ?

NINA.   Have you seen my wedding-ring ? I've hunted everywhere.

PEG.   You've lost it ?

NINA.   You know, dear, it was loose ; and I'm afraid it must have come off in the studio when I took off my glove. If the Prince should find it !

PEG.   He'll bring it here.

NINA.   What for ? He is no longer my friend, he is my enemy.

PEG.   Better that he should be !

NINA.   That man has been my evil genius, Peg ; but for him and Lady Coombe, I should never have got amongst the set I did.

PEG.   She is as much his dupe as you were.

NINA.   Yes, she lost more than I did. How right you were, dear, in all you said about him ! knowing what I do now, I can understand what would have been thought, if I had been found in his studio alone. But I'm not safe

yet. There's one thing that frightens me more than all—
I dread to think about it. Borowski has paid the money
I owed Lady Coombe.

PEG. How do you know?

NINA. He told me so.

PEG. Then he deceived you. It was Norman who
paid the Countess.

NINA. Norman!

PEG. Nina, you don't know how good he is. Why
don't you tell him everything?

NINA. If I had only told him at the first! (*sits on
sofa*, R.)

PEG. It isn't too late yet. He, too, has something to
confess.

NINA. What do you mean?

PEG. He will tell you himself. It is better *he* should
than I.

Enter TOM, L.

TOM. Good-morning!

PEG. Oh, Tom, you dear! Why didn't you come before? I thought of such a pretty speech just now to thank
you, and I declare it's all gone out of my head. (NINA
rises)

TOM. Never mind, Peg, you shall thank me presently
(*looking at* NINA), when nobody's looking. (*crosses to*
NINA) Is Norman at home?

NINA. No.

TOM. I'm sorry for that. I wanted to see him particularly.

PEG. You haven't come to see *me* then?

TOM. Well, I thought I could kill two birds with one
stone.

NINA *looks about meanwhile, then moves towards
door*, R.

PEG. (*curtseys*) Oh, thank you! but as this bird
objects to rude boys who throw stones, she'll fly away.
(*going*)

TOM. (*stopping her*) You're not going?

PEG. See! You've frightened Nina!

NINA. No, he hasn't, dear. (*aside to* PEG) I must
find the ring before Norman comes. (*exit*, R.)

PEG. Poor Nina! (*sits on settee*)

TOM. I'm glad she's gone. I've something to tell you

Peg, and I want to ask you whether you think I ought to tell Nina.

PEG. What is it?

TOM. They've had an extraordinary case at the Foreign Office lately. The Scotland Yard people have been to them, and this morning I had to go and make inquiries at one of the embassies. It is a queer case.

PEG. But whatever can it have to do with Nina?

TOM. I'll tell you. You remember, some time ago all the papers were full of a Greek fellow who called himself a Pashaw, got himself into the best society, set all the women to gambling, won no end of money, and turned out to be a mere adventurer.

PEG. Yes, I remember.

TOM. Well, this is just such another case ; and who do you think the distinguished foreigner is——

Enter SERVANT, L.

SERV. Prince Borowski! (PEG *rises*)

Re-enter PRINCE, L., *with cane ; exit* SERVANT, L. ;
TOM *gets back*, R.

PRINCE. Good-morning, Mees O'Reilly. Your sister is well this morning?

PEG. (*awkwardly*) Quite well, thank you. (*exit*, R.)

TOM. (*awkwardly*) How do you do? Good-morning. (*exit*, R.)

PRINCE. (*putting cane on table*, L.) *Qu'est-ce que cela veut dire? Hein!* Have they heard anything? Strange! I could have sworn I had seen that Frenchman's face before, who passed me in the street—but where? (*goes to window ; puts hat on table*, R.) Ah! (*staggers back*) I know him. He is of the French police. There they go. They have passed. Bah! Am I beginning to be a coward? I should have gone before —I have had warning enough—but I must have this money. I shall not leave that behind for my creditors. (*looking at cheque*) I want it myself. I should have seen it was crossed when I took it, and that I could not get the cash. He must give me an open one. I must put my head in the lion's mouth to get it. Bah! (*snaps fingers*) It is not the first time. (*watch*) Will he be long, I wonder? (*goes again to window*) I feel as if in a case since I have seen those Frenchmen. To-night I shall put the sea between me and England. (*re-enter* TREVANION) Good-morning. (L.)

TREV. (*starts; aside*) Borowski! (*aloud*) To what, sir, am I indebted for this visit?

PRINCE. A mere matter of business. I am leaving England to-day, and I have a crossed cheque of yours, for which I should be glad if you would give me an open one.

TREV. A cheque of mine!

PRINCE. For five hundred pounds. It is one that you gave Lady Coombe, and she has paid it to me.

TREV. (*aside*) Lady Coombe owes this man money?

PRINCE. I am going out of the country to-day, and it is not convenient for me in this form. (*holding out cheque*)

TREV. I have nothing to do with your convenience, and I must decline to interfere. My cheque was given to Lady Coombe, she accepted it, and there's an end of the matter.

PRINCE. It's not usual to decline so small a request made by one gentleman to another.

TREV. Doubtless! Had the request been made by one gentleman to another, I should have answered it differently.

PRINCE. Ah, you are courteous, Colonel Trevanion.

TREV. I didn't intend to be. (*goes up*)

PRINCE. Sir, you insult me! (*goes up*)

TREV. After what happened yesterday, your presence here is an insult to me.

PRINCE. There is nothing happened yesterday that can give you the right so to address me.

TREV. Mrs. Trevanion was at your studio.

PRINCE. I thought I had shown you, sir, that your suspicions were incorrect.

Re-enter NINA, R.

TREV. You only showed me that you were an adept in deception. *That*—my wife's glove—found in your studio by me proves you a liar. (*throws glove on sofa*)

NINA. (*aside*) My glove!

PRINCE. Do you throw down the glove that I may pick it up? (*picks it up*) Coward! Throw down your own! (*throws glove in* TREVANION'S *face*)

TREV. (*seizes* PRINCE'S *cane lying on table*) You cur! (NINA *rushes between them*)

TOM *and* PEG *re-enter*, R.

Ah, you protect him ?

NINA.   Yes, for even in anger he is not fit for you to touch.

SERVANT *re-enters* L.   TOM *crosses to her, she whispers to him ; he strolls back.   Exit SERVANT*, L.

PRINCE.   Madame !

NINA.   I have been your dupe too long, but I know you now for what you are—a thief !

PRINCE.   It is a lie !

TOM.   (*stepping between them*)   Oh no, it isn't.   Excuse my interrupting you, but there are two French gentlemen downstairs who wish to see you particularly.

TREV.   When I raised my hand to you, I forgot that you were in my house ; I remember it now.   (*goes to door*, L., *opens it*)   Leave it !   (*comes down*, L.)

PRINCE.   (*crosses to door*, L.)   Not yet, Colonel Trevanion.   You English are too cowardly to fight, except with your tongue, like the *canaille* that you are.   But I will fight you with your own weapons.   You call me thief —swindler ; what is *he ?*   (*turning on* TREVANION)   You have lived a lie before the world.   You have kept from this woman the secret of her birth that you might have the money that was another's.

NINA.   What does he mean ?

PRINCE.   (*turning to* NINA)   I mean that you had no right to your father's name or to his estates.

NINA.   (*crosses to* TREVANION, L.)   Norman, this is not true ?

PRINCE.   Do you know who you are, my proud lady ?

TREV.   She is my wife, and you shall not insult her.

PRINCE.   Your mother was an opera dancer, and your father was not her husband.

NINA.   Ah !   (*falls back in chair* L. *of* L. *table*)

TREV.   Be brave, Nina !   This was the mystery ; you know it now.

PRINCE.   The fortune you took with your wife was another's, and you know it.   There—(*points to* PEG)—is the lady you have defrauded.

TOM.   Peg !

PEG.   He has defrauded no one, and told me everything.   (*goes* R.)

PRINCE. It is very good of you to say so, Mees O'Reilly ;
I make you my compliments.

TOM. Keep your compliments, and take these ! (*hands*
PRINCE *his hat and cane*)

PRINCE. Thank you, Mr. Stanhope—(TOM *holds door
open,* L.) I congratulate you on your fortune—(*glancing
at* PEG)—or on so much of it as is left. (*at door,* L.)
Ladies, adieu ! pardon my abruptness in leaving you, but
my friends are impatient. (*exit,* L.)

TREV. How could I let him go ?

TOM. Don't trouble, Norman. He's already in the
hands of his impatient friends. (*at window,* L.)

NINA. Why was I not told of this before ?

TREV. The secret was not mine.

NINA. Was it kind—was it just—to keep it from me ?

TREV. It was your father's dying wish. I am a soldier ; he was my officer. It was his last command.

NINA. Then—when you married me, Norman, you
married——

TREV. The woman that I loved best in the world.

Re-enter MACADAM L., *followed by* JENKYN.

MAC. Come along, Jenkyn——

PEG. Ah, Mr. Macadam, back from Timbuctoo ?

MAC. Yes—I've brought Jenkyn with me. He's come
to apologize. (*aside*) Hang it ! I've had to double his
salary to make him do it.

JEN. (*to* TREVANION) Sir, I have just received a
visit from your solicitor !

TREV. Mr. Ogden !

JEN. And I am instructed by my proprietor, and on
his behalf, to apologize for this paragraph (*laying down
paper*) and any annoyance you may have been caused.
(TOM *takes up paper*)

TREV. But the apology must be published.

MAC. In the next number. I'll see to that.

TREV. In that case I'll take no further steps.

MAC. Thank you, my dear boy, thank you. (*shakes
hands with* TREVANION) You've let me off cheap, my
boy—dirt cheap !

TREV. You ! (*goes up to back,* L., *with* NINA)

ALL. You, Mr. Macadam !

MAC. The cat's out of the bag. I am the wretched
proprietor.

TOM. (*coming* C., *with paper*) I say, I've got a bone to pick with you.

MAC. Don't say there's anything about you in it?

TOM. Oh yes, there is.

JEN. About you, Mr. Stanhope? You don't say so?

MAC. We apologize! What is it?

TOM. Nothing libellous this time; only a breach of confidence.

MAC. Jenkyn, you're improving. There's a paragraph in the *Glass of Fashion* that isn't actionable.

JEN. Now, how on earth could that have got in?

TOM (*to* MACADAM) Read that! (*gives* MACADAM *paper*)

MAC. (*reads*) "It is whispered that a marriage" (PEG *gets to* C. *and looks over paper*) "has been arranged between the Hon. Tom Stanhope and the sprightly and accomplished Miss O'Reilly, sister of the beautiful Mrs. Trevanion." Well, my dear, we'll contradict it next week.

PEG. No, thank you! (*goes back* R. *with* TOM)

JEN. (*to* MACADAM) Dear me, I never saw that.

MAC. You don't want a *glass*. You want a pair of glasses.

LADY C. (*outside*, L.) Would you hold Horace? Thanks!

MAC. My wife! They'll tell her everything. (*hastily exits*, R.)

(*Enter* LADY COOMBE *with paper*, L.

LADY C. Has anybody seen Mr. Macadam?

PEG. Why, he was here just now. (TOM *goes off* R. *to fetch* MACADAM)

LADY C. I must find him. I won't rest until he has unearthed the proprietor of this scandalous publication.

JEN. My dear madame, I assure you you were not the beauty alluded to. I am a mere agent in the matter. If my apology is not sufficient— my proprietor, Mr. Macadam— Where is he?

LADY C. Mr. Macadam!

JEN. Oh, there you are!

Re-enter MACADAM *and* TOM, R.

LADY C. Macadam, you are the owner of this dreadful paper?

MAC. (*feebly*) I apologize!

LADY C.   The paper which has nearly been my ruin !

MAC.   You shall dictate the apology yourself.

TOM.   (*advancing to* LADY COOMBE)   Forgive him, Lady Coombe, Mr. Macadam's had quite enough of literature.

MAC.   Too much, my boy, too much !

LADY C.   Mr. Macadam !   We'll speak of this at home. (*goes up stage*)

MAC.   (*aside*)   I'd better have gone to Timbuctoo. (*joins* LADY COOMBE *up stage*)

NINA.   And you love me still ?

TREV.   I always loved you, Nina, and perhaps our future will be all the happier for the past.

NINA.   I have learnt my lesson.   From to-day I'll try and be more worthy of your love.

TREV.   Then for the second time—— (*shows ring*)

NINA.   My ring !

TREV.   With this ring I thee wed.

NINA.   For poorer this time, Norman, but for better. (*music*)

MAC.   (*coming down* C.)   Very well, my dear, I'll sell it.   Tom, do you want to buy a paper, to rule the social and the political world, and have society at your feet ?   If you do, I'll sell you the *Glass of Fashion*.   You shall have it cheap (*quick curtain*), dirt cheap !

CURTAIN.

www.ingramcontent.com/pod-product-compliance
Lightning Source LLC
Chambersburg PA
CBHW022032080426
42733CB00007B/807